Hearts Aren't Made of Glass

My Journey from Princess of Nothing to
Goddess of My Own Damned Life

a girl god publication

by Trista Hendren

©2016, All Rights Reserved

ISBN 978-1530925018

Printed in the United States

Cover Art by Arna Baartz

This book contains my recollections of my life as it happened, which—of course—will not please everyone. Some names and details have been changed or omitted to protect the privacy of others. My intention is not to hurt anyone, but to help other women who may find themselves in similar circumstances.

This book is dedicated to anyone who has been affected by alcoholism, addiction or abuse. It is my attempt to break the destructive cycle that plagued me for most of my life.

www.thegirlgod.com

Praise for Hearts Aren't Made of Glass

"Trista Hendren's story, grounded in the particular details of her life, transcends the personal, and beautifully. Trista models strength and tenacity, and truly heroic qualities to protect herself and her children. She candidly shares the hellish life she finally escaped to become an international leader in promoting the potential and safety of girls and women, which of course makes the world better for all humans."
-Donna J. Snyder, author of *The Tongue Has its Secrets*

"What a beautiful, honest and unusual book. Every page shattered and healed my heart."
-Laura Dodsworth, author of *Bare Reality*

"The story in this book touched the deepest part of my heart. Brave women are what keeps me going through life and Trista Hendren's bravery in telling her story in raw honesty made me feel honoured to be a woman. Every word told me that I can survive too." -Nicola O Hanlon, Recovery Writer

"We all reach that point where we have to rewrite the fairy tale template we were sold as children. If you are there, this book will make you feel less alone, while stirring up ideas that will help you, too, become the Goddess of your own damned life. Trista's story may have more or less dramatic upheavals than your own, but in this raw, unvarnished memoir you will find opportunities to rethink all those things you assumed were necessary—things as basic as your car and your particular creature comforts—while questioning how much of what we call privilege actually serves you. This is not a neatly wrapped up linear tale, but that is its beauty. It reads more like notes you'd scrawl in your journal. And you might want to have your own journal nearby as you read to write down the gems you will find in this memoir. I recommend this to anyone looking for women who have walked through the fire and come out glowing."
-Monette Chilson, author of *Sophia Rising*

Girl God Books

New Love: a reprogramming toolbox for undoing the knots

A powerful combination of emotional/spiritual techniques, art and inspiring words for women who wish to move away from patriarchal thought. This reprogramming toolbox combines the wisdom of intentional visual art and inspiring words. *New Love* includes a mixture of compelling thoughts and suggestions for each day, along with a "toolbox" to help you change the parts of your life you want to heal.

How to Live Well Despite Capitalist Patriarchy

This book will serve as a starting point to challenge some of our societal assumptions, in hopes of helping women become stronger and breaking their chains. As we begin to heal collectively, we can overturn this system altogether.

Original Resistance: Reclaiming Lilith, Reclaiming Ourselves

There is, perhaps, no more powerful archetype of female resistance than Lilith. As women across the globe rise up against the patriarchy, Lilith stands beside them, misogyny's original challenger. This anthology—a chorus of voices hitting chords of defiance, liberation, anger and joy—reclaims the goodness of women bold enough to hold tight to their essence. Through poetry, prose, incantation, prayer and imagery, women from all walks of life invite you to join them in the revolutionary act of claiming their place—of reclaiming themselves.

Inanna's Ascent: Reclaiming Female Power

Inanna's Ascent examines how females can rise from the underworld and reclaim their power, sovereignly expressed through poetry, prose and visual art. All contributors are extraordinary women in their own right, who have been through some difficult life lessons—and are brave enough to share their stories.

Re-visioning Medusa: from Monster to Divine Wisdom

A remarkable collection of essays, poems, and art: by scholars who have researched Her, artists who have envisioned Her, women who have known Her in their personal story, and then also combinations of all those capacities. All have spoken with Her and share something of their communion in this anthology.

Jesus, Muhammad and the Goddess
More than 35 International contributors reflect on finding Goddess within (and without) Christianity and Islam.

Whatever Works: Feminists of Faith Speak
A unique collection of writing by feminists of diverse faiths from around the world. This anthology combines personal essays, poems and academic musings with the goal of sparking conversations among women of all faith backgrounds—with the hope that we can find collective solutions to the global problems that plague women and girls living under patriarchy.

Single Mothers Speak on Patriarchy
More than 45 single mothers from around the world share their struggles and triumphs via essays, poems, art and critique.

The Abuse After the Abuse: How Men Use Money to Destroy Women
Co-authored by Trista Hendren and Angela Lee. Scheduled for 2019.

The Girl God
A book for children young and old, celebrating the Divine Feminine by Trista Hendren. Magically illustrated by Elisabeth Slettnes with quotes from various faith traditions and feminist thinkers.

Mother Earth
A loving tribute to Mother Earth and a call to action for children, their parents and grandparents. Written by Trista Hendren / Illustrated by Elisabeth Slettnes.

Tell Me Why
A feminist twist of the creation story told with love from a mother to her son, in hopes of crafting a different world for them both. Written by Trista Hendren / Illustrated by Elisabeth Slettnes.

Table of Contents

*"...it's been such a hard season, and the bridges
we burned might be all we had to keep us from drowning.
but at least we had this time; and i'd like to think
we're better off for it. i'll remember this.
sometimes broken things make the best
building supplies. and we'll keep on building.
hearts aren't made of glass, they're made of muscle,
and blood, and something else. and they don't
so much as break, as bend and tear.
we have what it takes to keep it together;
and move on."*
-Defiance, Ohio

When I became pregnant with an alcoholic, I should have known better. Throughout my pregnancy, he was *always* "running late." I worried whether he would even show up for the birth.

Fortunately, we were together—me on top, water bursting all over the bed—a month early.

We made it to the hospital just in time. I was already dilated to 10. Shortly after, he left to celebrate with friends—*just for a little while*. He returned late.

The next night, he didn't come back at all. The child screamed for hours. He had gas, but I didn't know it. I desperately called my first husband and his wife at 2 AM. They stayed with us until 5 AM, when my son was finally lulled to sleep.

Late that morning, he brought me an engraved Tiffany charm bracelet as an apology and left.

He was a spotty father for about a year before he disappeared completely. He came back—months later—*sorry.* He was always "sorry." When he went to rehab for several months, I had *hope.* When he stayed sober for a year, I married him against my better judgment and had another child.

There were three years of sobriety before it started again.

On our daughter's second birthday, we had nearly 50 people over to celebrate. Every time someone arrived, they asked where my husband was. Our five-year-old son had already begun to defend him. "Daddy's running late. There must be traffic."

My ex-husband turned on the grill and fed everyone. Six hours later, I finally broke down in hysteric sobs. *He never showed.* No one could console me. I knew it would never be "OK."

The next years went something like this: Confession. Three months at The Betty Ford Clinic; follow-up somewhere else. Al-Anon meetings. Relapse. Yelling, cursing, and pushing. Reading more books about his "disease." AA. More relapses. Therapy. Filing for bankruptcy; our home always on the brink of foreclosure. Confirmed affairs. Too many tears. 20 pounds lost. Dinner, cold on the table. Another missed birthday party. Children waiting, continuously waiting, on their little knees by the front window. He always claimed that he was, "Just around the corner." Dignity gone; children suffering. Me: alone, broke and striving to keep our "family" together.

I tried far too many times. He was always running late.

"How can someone tell you, 'I love you,' and then mistreat you and abuse you, humiliate you, and disrespect you? That person may claim to love you, but is it really love? If we love, we want the best for those we love."

-Don Miguel Ruiz, *The Mastery of Love*

My Name is Trista, *Princess of Nothing*

I liken living with an alcoholic to living in a war zone.

> *Like one who lives in deceit,*
> *I stone myself and call for help*
> *Your wound grows...*
> *It slits my throat from vein to vein.*
> -Hoda Al-Namani[1]

When I read this poem, I thought, this is *me*. This is *my* life.

Of course it was not *really* a war zone—and to suggest so seems a bit melodramatic—but it was a terrible and unpredictable life.

If you are a (male) addict, I'm sorry. This story isn't for or about you—unless you are sincerely interested in how it feels to be on the other side of things.[2]

---

[1] Al-Namani, Hoda."I Remember I was a Point, I was a Circle," translated from Arabic by Tim Mitchell.

[2] My belief is that males and females often abuse substances for different reasons, often with different results. As Gabor Maté wrote it *In the Realm of Hungry Ghosts*, "I don't have a single female patient in the Downtown Eastside of Vancouver who wasn't sexually abused...or abused, neglected and abandoned serially, over and over again."

Female addiction is beyond the scope of this book, however I highly recommend *Women, Sex, and Addiction: A Search for Love and Power* by Charlotte Davis Kasl, PhD , *Her Best-Kept Secret: Why Women Drink and How They Can Gain Control* by Gabrielle Glaser and *A Deeper Wisdom: The 12 Steps from a Woman's Perspective* by Patricia Lynn Reilly.

I have tried to balance what I have learned about addiction over these last 14 years with my strong belief in what Ellen Bass wrote: "Everyone has the right to tell the truth about her own life."

There are hundreds of stories and resources for addicts. This book is written for the families of addicts who are forgotten and who largely suffer in silence.

There will always be another excuse, another mistake, another relapse, another addiction—or anger about a parent's addiction—that they need their lifetime and yours to get over. With addicts there is just always *something*.

And, if you're reading this and you feel yourself getting angry—perhaps you probably know that someone is *finally* telling the truth.

Of course, I have empathy for addicts too. So much in fact that I stayed with one for seven years.[3]

When my husband first relapsed after his mother died, my well-meaning Christian father told me to "just love him." But that's the problem with addicts; the more you love, the more they take of you and everything else, until there's nothing left.

I remember the night I decided to stop walking on tiptoes.

I realized over the years I had become less of myself. I was worried about his anger, or that he would relapse. Suddenly I realized how ridiculous this all was. It was his turn to learn to deal with the reality of our existence instead of me having to shrink because of the reality of *his*.

I remember before the first rehab, a very good friend looked me straight in the eyes and said, "Run."

---

[3] I wrote this chapter many years ago and have softened considerably in my position since. That said, I felt it was important to keep the book in chronological order to show my own process of recovering from living with an addict.

My friend's mother had been an alcoholic and it had stunted his life. His comment affected our friendship for years. *I didn't want to run.* I thought I could fix my husband. I thought my love would be enough.

Four years later, when I found out about my husband's hidden relapse, I thought about this friend and the courage it took him to say this and acknowledge *my* reality.

While most other people tried to be polite—or pray for me—their comments seemed to gently gloss over what was actually happening. When someone doesn't fit into the perceived notion of what an addict is, it's hard for people to know what to say.

"Run" was the best advice I received and it's the advice I would give my daughter if she ever got involved with an addict.

Run. Run like hell.

The reason this advice hurt so much at the time was that it would have forced me to see my part in things. And when you are with an alcoholic, you are used to suffering in silence as the martyr, wondering why the alcoholic does what he does.

I wasted years of my life wondering *why.* I've come to realize it doesn't matter.

Running would have taken courage. It would have said, "He cannot do this to me. I am stronger than this. I can do better." Instead, I stayed w—a—y too long.

Leaving would have forced me—and others—to acknowledge the truth.

Alcoholism remains hidden in the shadows. Very few people are willing to talk about it. We go to great lengths to avoid the subject altogether. Both the addict and the co-dependent will do anything to hide their sense of inadequacy. There is nobody that tries harder at being "normal" than an alcoholic and his family.

If I ran away, I would have to tell the truth. He drinks—*all the time*. It is not pleasant. He is verbally abusive. *My life is out of control*. And the hardest truth: *I need help*.

When I finally left my husband, I was only able to do so after taking weeks to compose a list of facts. At my office, I began to put together a list of the things in our relationship that I could not accept. This included that he did not go to my grandfather's funeral, he did not come home all night long, and he brought cocaine into our home. After four and half pages of undeniable facts, I realized that there was no longer any question of whether or not I could stay with him. The list made that impossible, even laughable.

When you live with an addict, you are never quite certain about reality. Everything becomes blurred. By writing down the facts as they happened, he could not come back to me later with his own version of the truth.

In my case, there were months of lying about his sobriety when I just wasn't sure whether he was drinking or not. Had I begun the list sooner, instead of listening to the words I so wanted to believe, I would have saved myself at least a year of heartbreak.

Before I left my husband, a dear friend sent me a quote from Maya Angelou. It said, "When someone shows you who they are, believe them—the first time!" As women, we must remember to trust our instincts and not wait for the people in our lives to change.

The truth is, I knew what I thought of my ex the first time I met him, but I gave him chance after chance despite it.

While I have seen some wonderful transformations in Alcoholics Anonymous, the statistics are not promising and I would not place any bets for my future on another addict.

There are millions of kind and addiction-free wo/men in the world.

I happen to now be married to one of them.

"Remember pain. Your pain is your key to freedom...
and when we speak, the pain dissolves
into a river of tears where it belongs."
-SARK

Once upon a time I married a man with a rich family. I remember Dr. Phil saying, "If you marry rich, you'll earn every nickel"—but I thought that didn't apply to me because I didn't care about their money. I figured I'd make my own money as I always had. I didn't realize then that making money as a single person is much easier that making money as a single mom with two small children.

Because I am a family person, I treated my in-laws kindly and gave them the sort of considerations I gave my own family. I suppose this gave the presumption that I would be easily controlled.

On the eve of my wedding night, my father-in-law ruined the rehearsal dinner by ranting and raving at our table about the service. At one point he even turned to my soon-to-be-husband and I and asked, "How long do we have to stay at your wedding tomorrow?" I felt like telling him not to come at all. The rest of us were enjoying our dinner but it soon become impossible with him there. I suppose he thought he was entitled to do this because he was paying for dinner. I left in tears after having words with my groom. I stayed up most of the night wondering if I could marry into this family. I wondered if my soon-to-be husband would turn into his father.

I didn't like the way my father-in-law treated people. I didn't like the way he made me feel. I had a horrible feeling in the pit of my stomach that I didn't get over all night and well into the morning. All my bridesmaids were at my house and we talked it over at length with no real conclusions. Finally I just asked to be alone. I stayed up well past 3 AM thinking and re-thinking the entire situation.

At around 10 AM, my father-in-law called to apologize. I can't remember now what he said but in many ways, I wish I hadn't taken the call. It was the beginning of a pattern: his very bad, unfathomable ranting behavior, followed by an apology.

My father-in-law didn't let the rehearsal dinner go for months. He had told me I could choose the venue, and I had with great care. We went to Ricardo's: a beautiful Italian restaurant where I been lunching for more than 10 years. Because of the service he *thought* we received, he hassled the owner for months over a $250 fee that we all knew he had agreed to pay ahead of time. It was embarrassing to me to say the least. Ricardo ended up just refunding his money to get him off his back. My father-in-law called me to gloat about it. I got that sick feeling in my gut again. I went back to Ricardo's and apologized. Ricardo was so gracious to me, but I also felt he knew the obvious now too. *I was screwed.*

There was a brief honeymoon period for all of us after I became pregnant with our second child. I tried to give my new in-laws the benefit of the doubt. I made excuses for very bad behavior. I was often uncomfortable—but they were "family."

My husband had been in therapy the six years that I'd known him and in and out of rehab since he was 15. I found it progressively harder to fault my husband and angered more and more at my in-laws for raising him this way. I never grew up with money so I never expected anything from anybody. What was worse was I didn't want anything from the in-laws I was growing increasingly uncomfortable with. I found that there were several occasions that I had unknowingly benefited from their "goodwill." It was always rubbed in my nose later in some way.

This was ironic because I was actually a single mother raising their first grandchild by myself for more than a year and rarely received a nickel from anyone—or even an offer to baby-sit for that matter. My husband's drinking was out of control and left me pretty much on my own.

His father once went so far as to announce that my husband and I were *poor* in front of their guests at a dinner party. Again, I was baffled. I had earned an MBA in the evenings in my mid-twenties and was making what I considered to be a very good living for my age. I wasn't exactly up to his standards, but *poor*?

They were the type that always gave us their gifts with the price tags still on—even though (despite their wealth) the gifts usually were unwrapped markdowns of markdowns from Target or some other outlet mall store. There never seemed to be any consideration in the gift giving. In fact, his wife once even re-gifted me the favor from my wedding within that very same year. And not to be sweet or sentimental; she really had no idea.

My father-in-law's wife told me the best thing that could happen to my husband's brother, who was institutionalized with a mental illness, was for him to *die*. Within the same week, she told me the same thing about my husband's mother, who he happened to adore. I noticed her tone often changed when she was alone with me. It wasn't that happy Country Club voice she used around other people. It was cold and sharp. I would back away from her, but she would draw me in again with the sweet voice—only to surprise me later with her sharp sentiments when I least expected them.

Then the unthinkable happened. My husband's mother did die—suddenly, and with many things left unsaid. My husband's three years of sobriety went out the window. He started drinking again, secretly. He became a very different (and abusive) person.

I made the mistake of going to my father-in-law for help. He had been sober for more than 20 years, and I thought he could understand my plight. But that call for help seeped into every area of my life. He and his wife thought they had the right to comment on and criticize every aspect of my life, my marriage and how I raised my children. And that is when the gloves came off between my in-laws and me.

My father-in-law told me, "This is war!" Granted, this is a 60-year-old, successful (and well respected) man. How do you respond to someone like this? He, of course, apologized a few days later. At the time I felt sorry for him. I told him that I didn't think that anyone had ever really been honest with him because of his money and that I was going to tell him the truth.

I soon suspected that he and his wife felt entitled to do or say anything because their money made them "better" than everyone else. They began to criticize nearly everything I did—even though I was the one taking care of their two grandchildren while their son was out on another relapse.

Worse yet, it did not matter that they both admittedly had drinking problems while they were raising their own children. In my mind, most of my husband's problems stemmed back to the lack of care he received while he was growing up. *What did they know?*

One night, my husband arrived home late and acted very strange. He had spent the weekend with some friends. We watched Mitch Album's *For One More Day* and he burst into sobs. He would not tell me what was wrong, but I knew it was *bad*. My husband went upstairs to the spare bedroom and quickly fell into a deep sleep. I could not wake him. I started to fume, and then realized something was very off.

I decided to search his things. I found three folded-up magazine pages in his coat pocket. When I opened one, white powder spilled all over our one-year-old daughter and me. The dust blew into my mouth; I inhaled some through my nose. I started shaking and became hysterical. I was still unable to wake up my husband. My son, fortunately, was already asleep.

I called my father-in-law sobbing, desperate for help. He told me it was "not a big deal" and instructed me to flush the cocaine down the toilet. I argued with him. I told him I thought I should call the police. He questioned why my daughter was still up. He shouted, "I don't care if you get any sleep or not. You put her to bed!"

I told him, "I didn't call you for parenting advice; I called you because your son is using cocaine." I hung up the phone.

I made a few more phone calls and ultimately decided to call the police. My mother came so that the children would not see anything. The police told me to lock myself in my bedroom in case he became violent. My husband was arrested and put in jail.

My father-in-law called approximately 20 times the next day, but I didn't answer. I didn't want to talk to him, but I vented and cried. I wrote a poem about the night, and how he made me feel like "a nobody." I made the mistake of sending it to him.

He responded by email a few days later, writing that he "told me what to do and I did something else that was so stupid I probably ruined our relationship and my marriage."

I stopped talking to him.

Once upon a time I thought I married a boy with giant green eyes and a bigger heart. I thought that together we could overcome his addictions and his past.

I was dead wrong.

I also married his dysfunctional family and they almost swallowed us all whole.

When my grandfather died soon afterward, everything was put back into perspective. While he passed with far less than a million dollars in the bank, he was truly one of the happiest and contented people I've ever met. He never worried about what other people were doing. He never once put me down or made me feel bad about myself. He adored my children, and they adored him. There were never any strings attached to his love.

My grandfather's death, while extremely painful, also gave me courage and a pathway to great reflection. *I had settled.* My grandparents had everything in the world that I had ever wanted —and in most people's minds, that was probably very little. However, a life embodied in love *is* a rich one.

I also came to realize that I was, as they say, *the author of my own life*. My in-laws were just really bad characters that needed to be written out of it.

"We have been raised to fear the yes within ourselves, our deepest cravings. But, once recognized, those which do not enhance our future lose their power and can be altered. The fear of our deepest cravings keeps them suspect and indiscriminately powerful, for to suppress any truth is to give it strength beyond endurance. The fear that we cannot grow beyond whatever distortions we may find within ourselves keeps us docile and loyal and obedient, externally defined, and leads us to accept many facets of our own oppression as women."

-Audre Lorde

Shortly after our second wedding anniversary, my husband and I were invited to an extended weekend at the Four Seasons outside of San Diego. I left our kids at home with my mother and flew down to meet him. My husband was already there, after several days of business in LA. It should have been a clue to me that he sent a driver instead of picking me up himself. *He was golfing.* While it annoyed me, I didn't want it to ruin our time together. So I put my angst on the back burner.

We stayed in a two-bedroom suite as guests of our friend Trevor from Beverly Hills. It was a high-end timeshare of some sort that Trevor's parents owned. Trevor wears makeup and takes bubble baths. He annoys me, but he's completely lovable in his own way.

My husband is a recovering alcoholic. He's been in recovery now for three years but his mother just died and our friend committed suicide and then my grandpa got sick right after that. After caring for my grandpa for six weeks in his home, he died too. I'm not so sure my husband is sober anymore, but whenever I ask him he says he is. *He swears he is.*

The first part of the trip wasn't so bad. We ate well, sat by the pool, and actually had sex (a small miracle with two young children). But then more people joined us.

We sit and talk on our balcony alone for a while. My husband seems giddy. *Is he drunk?* I never seem to be able to catch him drinking. He doesn't slur his words, but there have been times when he does not come home, and other times when he is very mean. My husband is not a mean person when he is sober.

We talk about our life, and our plans. Things seem hopeful. He seems happy. He says he wants to do things different. He has been working a lot. I barely see him lately. I am glad to hear these words, but I am hesitant. *Is he drunk?* Is this too good to be true?

After a nice Italian dinner, and many, many drinks, the bill comes and none of our *affluent friends* seem to have any money. After hours of hearing all the details of their personal wealth, my husband is left with another large tab. We roll eyeballs at each other as he hands over the American Express card.

I confront Trevor about the drinking while my husband takes over the piano bar, singing some Sinatra song. Trevor says he may have had *a few beers* earlier. I am agitated, but decide to wait until we are alone to speak to him. On the ride home, he becomes belligerent. By the time we reach the hotel, we are openly engaged in a nasty fight. The couple driving us tries to intervene, but it is useless.

And this is where it gets hazy. I'm not sure what is real, what is remembered, what is embellished, what has been blocked, and when I went completely over the edge.

Back at the resort, I asked my husband about whether he is drinking again. This time he admits it. He grabs a bottle of tequila in the kitchen and nearly guzzles the whole thing. I am hysterical. I beat his chest, or maybe it is the wall, or the bed or the pillow. We are screaming. Trevor comes in and begs us to stop. He says he is *traumatized*. He says that everyone can hear us—reminding us that it is his parent's place.

Trevor takes his Ambien and makes himself a drink. I am crying and not making any sense. My husband leaves the room for something and I lock him out. I start calling people, basically anyone, hysterical, and drunk myself. The AA people must think I'm completely nuts. I cry all night in heavy sobs. I wonder what will become of our life. I don't know how I could have been so stupid. I am angry for believing a lie that was so obvious. I *wanted* to believe it. *A relapse was so inconvenient for me*.

At some point I unlock the door and let my husband back in. We are both still angry. I am unable to get out of bed the entire next day. I cannot come to terms with my life. I decide to tell my husband that I will not leave him if he gets sober. *As if* he could just stop right then, and it would all be over, and we could go back to our neat little life.

Trevor knocks on the door to settle the bill early in the morning. I wouldn't look at him or him at me. My head hurts and I want to die, *literally*. He doesn't have any money, but he won't say this in front of me, so my husband has to go into the other room with him. When we leave, we see one of the other couples from dinner —the people who drove us home. We mutually ignore each other. The plane ride home is silent.

I wish I could say that it was one night that determined the course of my life forever and everything got better from there. But life is never that obvious. It was a hangover of that night, a relapse that went on for more than a year before my husband finally went to treatment. But it was the residue from that day that caused me to see my own part in things.

A happy marriage is not handed to you. A good life does not happen by itself (usually). But somehow I lived most of my life waiting for someone else to make everything right for me and got mad when that didn't happen.

That day was a kick in the head, a slap in the face—telling me to wake up. Addiction runs on both sides of our families and I was in no position to be complacent with two small children. I had to deal with my own co-dependency issues. I had to finally look at what had brought me to marry an addict after escaping a childhood plagued by addiction myself.

I do not know why that day took a year to manifest. *It was the worst year of my life.* I found cocaine in my home and separated from my husband. I refused my own birthday party. I stopped talking to my in-laws. My sister's lover died from complications of ALS and then my husband's stepbrother took his own life.

I had resisted AA and Al-Anon because I hated the concept that I was not in control of alcoholism. But in truth, we are in control of *nothing*.

Perhaps growing up with addicts had prohibited me from being able to see things as they are. I never learned to trust my own reality. *I never knew I was even entitled to one.*

I needed a year of harsh realities because that one day did not wake me up from my self-inflicted coma. But on that day I vowed that I would never drink that much again. And, I vowed that I would *always* speak my truth.

I spent a lot of time reading. I spent a lot of time reflecting. I spent a lot of time fighting—learning how to defend myself. For a long time, I had put up with too much. *I had been silent.* I wanted things to go smoothly, but silence never willed them that way.

All I wanted that day was to put my head under the covers and disappear, but life with children does not give you that luxury. *I had to go home.* I am grateful I did not have the option to tune out—for the slap in the face that made me realize that this was *my life* waiting for me to wake up and be present.

"A society which beggars its mothers beggars its own future."

-Ann Crittenden

Inhumane.

That is what being a single mother felt like after my husband left our house.

Dr. Suess says, "alone is something you'll be quite a lot"—and that is something I feel all the time now. I am alone. I am exhausted. I am fuming inside all the time and occasionally this spills over onto these two small children who I absolutely adore.

Unfair. That is how it feels. My two-year-old runs around saying, "I am angry. I am sad. I am not OK." My five-year-old kicks her in the gut hard. He says it is because he is angry that his dad is gone.

Sometimes I feel we live like animals. Mostly I feel my ex is an animal for leaving us this way. For his fucking booze and the cocaine he still won't admit to after all this time.

Inhumane.

No one offering to help me with these children other than my mother. The exhaustion that creeps in every day. The chores that don't stop. The bills that don't stop. My to-do list that only seems to grow.

Inhumane.

Another single mom tells me, "Sometimes I just say yes because they just keep asking and asking and asking—and I am just too tired to say anything else and I just cannot take it anymore." Her kids are older than mine, and I think, *this is what I have to look forward to.*

I see a mother at the doctor's office speaking to her children in that fake "mother voice" and I think at least—I hope—that I am always *real* with my children. At least I have not come to *that*. But then I think, *isn't it sad that I even have to wonder?* I am not sure of anything anymore.

Inhumane.

The looks I get from people when I am with my children when I don't wear my six carats of wedding rings. *Yes,* it changes things. *Substantially*.

Inhumane.

I am now wearing a size zero. I have become a zero. This wasn't supposed to happen to me—I look like Catherine Zeta-Jones for God's sake—at least that's what everyone always told me before I started disappearing. I don't know who I am anymore or where I am going or especially *how the fuck* I got here. I have an MBA. I was making a good salary. I bought my home on my own. I did all the things I thought I was supposed to do. This wasn't the plan. This wasn't the life I thought I would have.

But here I am. *A single mother*. And it just feels *inhumane* and wrong.

The sad thing is that I know that I am one of the *lucky* ones. I am *privileged*. I at least have *some* money.

But whenever I think of my situation, or what is happening to my children now, only one word comes to mind...

Inhumane.

"When nurturing children is truly valued, mothers who work at home will be economically protected and men will want to join us as equal partners in parenting."

-Harriet Lerner, *The Mother Dance*

When I thought I was happily married, it seemed I could do no wrong. Everyone told me what a *good* mother I was and how well I managed my home and job and family. Now people often tell me, condescendingly, "You're doing the best you *can*."

When I realized my husband was a no good drunk who had been lying to me for well over a year and that even my own life was a complete lie, I decided I had to change. But change was harder than I thought it would be.

When you make a commitment to someone, you build a life— even if that life just consists of stories you tell yourself in your head. I became a teary-eyed crazy person that I even hated to be around. I felt like less of a person without my wedding ring on— without a husband.

I tried to read every self-help book I could find for 5-6 months, and that worked for a while. But I soon realized that *nothing was changing*. My life was still a mess, and no matter how I tried to hypnotize myself otherwise, it would probably be a mess for a while.

The worst part about starting over is that you are vulnerable, and everyone still feels the need to give you advice. It feels like criticism. *Everything* feels like criticism and you are already so raw that it is just too much.

I realized that trying to date would never work for me. My children were two and five, and they still slept with me most nights. They were also anxious and upset much of the time—and I was too. I quickly realized that it was going to be a long time before I was ever going to be ready to let someone else in.

In reality, I didn't really want to start over. I knew that my husband had lied—and probably cheated—among other things. And, while this sounds terrible, I just wanted to be a wife and mother and not have to worry about money, where to live, how to live, what to do, or any of the major choices that I thought I had already made years prior. Despite how miserable I was, I just somehow couldn't get the mojo to file for divorce. I left it hanging over my head like a noose.

I was depressed and I didn't know how not to be depressed anymore. My friend told me to let myself feel it, and I did. But I wondered how long I would feel this way and if it would ever lift. I wondered what kind of mother I was to my children and if they were suffering because I was. It was easier to be angry, but I couldn't seem to muster anger anymore. I decided to forgive my husband, and then the only person I was able to be angry at anymore was *myself*.

I wanted to have a good life. I thought I had one. *What happened?* How did I go from one thing to another so quickly?

"I will not have my life narrowed down.
I will not bow down to somebody else's whim
or to someone else's ignorance."

-bell hooks

The costs of other people's addictions have been too high for me. Alcoholism cost me my maternal grandfather. He died much too young, much too sad, and much too angry. There were no more ice cream sundaes after school, no more Hostess Ding Dongs, and no more long talks about life.

My maternal grandfather was a functioning alcoholic. He was a very hard-worker and always took care of his family. I was not prepared for the non-functioning version of alcoholism—where everything just *stops* and life turns completely upside down.

Of course, adding drugs into the mix intensifies things. Had I known cocaine was involved, I never would have gone anywhere near my husband. Drugs have always terrified me.

My husband's addictions have stopped me from doing so many things I love these last seven years. I used to travel the world. I have not been out of the country since I met my husband.

I have been stuck in so many ways—*paralyzed,* really. I have stopped seeing friends I adore nearly as often because I am often sad. I feel *alone.*

I used to have parties all the time. I loved them. When my husband got sober, I stopped drinking altogether so I wouldn't temp him. Then I stopped having parties altogether—except one big party a year. I felt like it would be *too much* to have all these people having fun all around him. I felt like I had to protect his sobriety. Now I realize that *I* missed out. He relapsed anyway and was out having his own parties while I was sitting at home with two small children.

But I think mostly what this relationship has cost me is the freedom to be myself. As painful as it is to watch the ones you love stuck in their addictions, it is more painful to look at the choices you have made as an individual because you felt stuck.

"No matter what you say in all your anger and brokenness and rage, it's not mine to keep, it's not mine to carry, and I won't."

-Isa Elmazoski

My husband forgot to put away his Betty Ford workbook and I came across it this afternoon. I actually had seen it hidden away in a drawer in the garage several months ago but didn't look through it then.

It seemed odd to me that it was out. Almost like he left it there on purpose. When I asked him about it later, he said he had taken it out to take to the condo. There are multiple places he could have kept the book—like the box he keeps at the bank that he doesn't think I know about.

In any case, I read through it.

I have always suspected that my husband has had affairs. But I have never been able to prove it. I think you know in your heart when someone is unfaithful to you.

I have asked him about it point blank numerous times. But he always denied it to the hilt. He acted like I am completely crazy for even thinking it—*even when he stayed out all night.*

But what I have found now confirms it.

In a lot of ways, I am just relieved to finally know the truth. There is something very liberating about that.

But in another way, I am very angry that he lied about it and did not tell me sooner.

I was ready to file for divorce two years ago. I went to see an attorney then, but he convinced me to wait and try to work it out.

Had I known about the depth of his addictions, I would have made different choices. I wasn't in this financial mess then. I could have walked away and been done and today would be completely different for me.

It's not just the infidelity. It is the lies. It is everything else. There were three women. *He had unprotected sex with three different women.*

I know specifically who one of them is. It's funny because she was always the one I had suspected before. He told me when she started using cocaine again; I was suspicious as to why he started talking to her then since he was "working his program." He said he was trying to help her get sober, but that didn't ring true to me.

I thought about just holding onto everything and not letting my husband know about the journal, but I *couldn't*. He called about half an hour after I read everything and I was still fuming.

So I told him I had read it. And I also told him I had read all the parts about him driving drunk with our children in the car and putting us all at risk in *that way* too.

I suppose I expected him to take responsibility and say he was deeply sorry. Instead, he called me a "miserable cunt."

"The wounded child inside many males is a boy who, when he first spoke his truths, was silenced by paternal sadism, by a patriarchal world that did not want him to claim his true feelings. The wounded child inside many females is a girl who was taught from early childhood that she must become something other than herself, deny her true feelings, in order to attract and please others. When men and women punish each other for truth telling, we reinforce the notion that lies are better."

-bell hooks, *All About Love: New Visions*

I realized the other day that I am still waiting for my fairy tale to come true. And looking at my life and all the others around me I *should have* realized a long time ago that was never going to happen. I need to take control of my own life.

And I need to consider the impact of all the Barbie and Princess books my daughter loves so much will have on her life.

My daughter is a VERY strong girl. Truly, I wish I had her strength. But I wonder what our culture will squelch in her—and what impressions my own life has made on her.

This is a hard thing for me. I consider myself a feminist and earned a Women Studies minor in college. And yet, my own upbringing was very traditional. While it wasn't always happy, I have found myself striving for that same model in my adult life—even when there was never a chance of that working out long-term.

I've told several of my younger friends not to ever give up their financial independence. I still wish I had not done that. But it is also such a trade-off—and one I wish no one had to make.

I have enjoyed my kids, thoroughly. I am still saddened by the first year of my son's life. I was working way too much.

Sometimes I almost feel like I want to have another baby—not because I want another baby per say, but just so I can somehow recapture that time.

But the truth is, that time is gone and I have to make my peace with it.

I remember an exercise my counselor tried with me many years ago about seeing things as they are instead of how we want them to be. I don't think I was ready for that then. But I'm slowly beginning to see that I need to be ready now.

"I have been in Sorrow's kitchen and licked out all the pots. Then I have stood on the peaky mountain wrapped in rainbows, with a harp and a sword in my hands."

-Zora Neale Hurston

I've thought about this quote a lot lately. I've read enough and seen enough of the world to know that, often, there are no happy endings. A *happy ending* is an American ideal, and it doesn't work out for a lot of people, *including Zora*.

The fighting keeps escalating between my husband and me. There seems to be little peace. He texts me 50-100 times a day, and calls at least 8-20 times a day. I have decided to ignore him. There is little point in responding now.

He refuses to give us any money, even when he promises he will. Only if something is *dire*—like the cable or electricity are about to be shut off—will he pay the bill directly. He thinks he is justified because, thus far, he is paying for the kids' private school tuition. I suppose that makes all sorts of sense to him because it strokes his ego to know his kids are attending the best schools in our area— and he gets to socialize with all the rich people he cares so much about.

But what good is private school if you can't feed your kids or pay your basic bills? It makes no sense to me. I'm glad my kids can attend good schools. I think education is important. *But not like this*.

I do not believe he has any intention of settling this peacefully or respectfully anymore.

Yesterday, we were supposed to meet at our gym at 1 PM. He called me after 1 and said he was running late. I continued my work out. (The kids were in the supervised play room waiting for their dad to pick them up.)

He started sending me nasty texts so I ignored him. I went to check on the kids about an hour later and he had not showed up. They asked me why their dad didn't pick them up. I told them I didn't know. I took them swimming. The nasty texts continued.

Next, my husband told me that he had taken our little Yorkie, Gus. He said he'd meet us and give us the dog if I gave him the kids.

While initially Gus was a Christmas gift for my husband, he's never shown any concern for him before—except as a bargaining tool. When I was pregnant with our son, I threatened to leave him because of his drinking. He told me if I did, he would take the dog with him.

Being pregnant with an alcoholic partner who sometimes does not bother to come home is pure hell. I remember crying myself to sleep many nights while I was pregnant. That dog was my only solace. At that point in my life I rarely called anyone for help. I would just lay there crying and snuggling Gus until I fell asleep.

I remember his threat so vividly. I wish I had left then. It's the same bullshit now except there are two kids involved.

My daughter uses the dog for solace too. She walks around every room in the house carrying Gus. She adores him. He is her comfort, as he used to be mine.

I warned the kids before we arrived home that Gus would not be there. I was not about to give my husband the satisfaction of an emotional breakdown from any of us. I thought they were OK, but then my daughter woke up screaming with a nightmare about her dog being gone. It took a while to get both kids back to sleep and then I laid there for about an hour before I fell asleep.

"Risk! Risk anything! Care no more for the opinions of others, for those voices. Do the hardest thing on earth for you.
Act for yourself. Face the truth."

-Katherine Mansfield

Last night I started thinking of the purpose of my writing, and *the purpose of my life really.*

I want to raise healthy, addiction-free children.

All of my time and investment is in achieving this goal. And at times I resent my husband and father-in-law, but I don't want that to cloud my true purpose.

It seems it is more important to them to demonize me and protect their money than to focus on these kids.

Next week, I will go back to work full-time. I have been gradually working toward that these last few weeks, but next week, both kids will be in school for 5-6 hours a day. My mother has (again) stepped forward and offered to help in huge ways that I will never be able to repay.

It is going to be a huge adjustment for all of us—and at times I feel very sad and bitter about it. I don't want my 3-year-old in school for so long. It seems *way* too young to me. But it seems there is no other option now.

I'm realizing more and more that I really enjoy the peaceful life without my husband. I want a relaxed and drama-free life. Bring him into the picture, and there is always intense negativity.

I am increasingly certain that I want a divorce.

I don't know how to accomplish that financially. I feel

overwhelmed with our existing obligations, and I know very well that most of that will not be something I can maintain on my own —or even walk away from without a lot of problems.

That said, I also need to finally acknowledge (and accept) that my husband screwed us financially and I have waited years for him to "fix it." But things are only getting worse.

I'm going to have to walk away from something.

I need to figure out a way to support the kids and myself. I don't know what that will be at this point, but there has to be some way.

"Recovery"

"I am no longer accepting the things I cannot change.
I am changing the things I cannot accept."

-Angela Davis

Tomorrow is the start of school, and I cannot sleep. I am very upset about my daughter starting school on an all-day basis. It just breaks my heart. I started thinking about the passage on acceptance from "The Big Book."

> "And acceptance is the answer to all my problems today. When I am disturbed, it is because I find some person, place, thing, or situation—some fact of my life— unacceptable to me, and I can find no serenity until I accept that person, place, thing, or situation as being exactly the way it is supposed to be at this moment. Nothing, absolutely nothing happens in God's world by mistake. Until I could accept my alcoholism, I could not stay sober; unless I accept life completely on life's terms, I cannot be happy. I need to concentrate not so much on what needs to be changed in the world as on what needs to be changed in me and my attitudes."

I can accept that this is the only choice I have for my daughter right now. What is hard to accept is that it is the selfish actions of her father that has brought us here. That I *can't* accept; I don't know if I will ever be able to.

My daughter is three years old. We can never get this precious time back. I feel like it is being robbed from me. I feel like her happy little spirit is being robbed from her. And I am very, very angry about that.

Earlier today my husband wanted to stop by to get some things and I became upset. Why do we always have to change our plans to accommodate him? *When does he ever accommodate us?*

I told him not to come. I am tired of having my children's lives upset and turned upside down. I am tired of him *pretending* to be a father. I am tired of having anything at all to do with him.

His stuff has been here for five months. There should be no sudden urgency about anything anymore. All he left us with is a bunch of old junk.

I know the passage about acceptance has worked for people. There is just very little I feel like accepting right now.

I re-watched "Malcolm X" the other day and thought, *there is a man who didn't live by the status quo or accept the bullshit that was handed to him*. And they killed him.

Sometimes I wonder if life for the "successful" is just a puppet dance. Playing by someone else's rules that really don't work for you.

Somewhere in all of this I need to find what does work—for me, and for my children.

"When it comes to *women*, how far do patriarchal and exploitative capitalist values *rely* on women providing *unwaged* care, on which our society can freeload and from which it can wash its hands of financial responsibility?"

-Vanessa Olorenshaw

Today was my first "official" full day back at work. Not that I have not been working. I have been. But I have also been taking care of two young children, a house, and a husband that apparently doesn't give a fuck about any of us. I have continued to work as a mortgage broker for the last 12 years. I do not make the 6-figure salary I once made, but I have always contributed.

That said, I feel my most significant contribution is raising my children. There is no value in that in my husband's family, but to me that is the most valuable thing.

Today was a difficult day to say the least. Not as difficult as yesterday, but hard as hell. My daughter hates it when I leave her. She cries and holds on to my legs. I literally have to pick her up and pass her off to someone else so that I can walk out the door while she cries.

My new day will consist of getting up hours before what I would even like to think about and spending an hour-and-a-half driving both children to school before I start work. My husband will never understand what it takes to wake two young children up while it is dark out, get them cleaned up, dressed, fed, lunches packed and out the door on time to make three deadlines—two different school start times, and one for me at work. Repeat again at the end of the day.

Nevertheless, my soon-to-be ex-husband had the audacity to ask me, "Why aren't you making any money?"

Let me explain something. As a mortgage broker, I get paid on commission. *Only* commission.

Once I get a call that someone wants a loan, I am lucky if that loan closes within 30-60 days. Then, I get paid on the loan, about half of what the loan fee is, within about a month.

I sent out a letter letting my clients and friends know that I am back to working full-time 2-3 weeks ago.

The reason I am back to work full-time—instead of raising these kids like I would like to be doing—is that my husband quit working entirely for more than a year.

Meanwhile... I was working, doing everything around this house, and taking care of our children. And taking care of children who have emotional outbursts because of their absent father is *completely different* than taking care of children with another fully functional adult.

None of this should be news to my husband. I have been working as a commissioned loan officer since before I met him.

So I asked my husband, "Why haven't YOU been making any money?"

And then he said, "I don't want to argue."

Then the pipe burst in our bathroom while the kids were taking their evening bath and, like last time, my husband is no where to be found. So the hot water squirted into my face and all over the floor and onto the kids. I had to have my 6-year-old-son hold down the faucet so I could put some clothes on and go outside to turn off the water supply to the entire house.

So now we have no water.

"Grandfather-Grandmother, look at our brokenness.
We know that in all creation only the human family has
strayed from the Sacred Way. We know that we are the ones
who are divided and we are the ones who must come back
together to walk in the Sacred Way. Grandfather, Grandmother,
Sacred One, teach us love, compassion, and honor that we
may heal the earth and heal each other."

-Ojibway Prayer

I'm tired of Al-Anon. I realized today in my meeting that I just wasn't feeling it. I still like the literature and I will probably go back. But today I feel like it's all the same story over and over again. *When* are we all going to move on with our lives and be happy?

There is a girl in there that reminds me so much of my daughter. My daughter looks a lot like me, but somehow this girl with the Russian accent is so much like my daughter to me. I sat next to her once and it was almost overwhelming for me. I had tears in my eyes throughout the whole meeting. *There is something about her spirit.* I haven't seen her for a long time but she was there today. The same feeling came back to me when I saw her during the prayer at the close of the meeting.

> *God grant me the serenity*
> *to accept the things I cannot change,*
> *the courage to change the things I can,*
> *and the wisdom to know the difference.*

I don't want my kids to end up in a 12-step program. I don't want them to be addicts *or* co-dependents. Even the *thought* of it is overwhelmingly sad for me.

It seems like there has to be a better alternative to all of this.

Maybe if I raise my kids with these principles they will be better for it. I just don't want them to have the life I've had—or the life my husband has had.

I spoke to my maternal grandma early in the week about Al-Anon. She was married to my alcoholic grandpa for 36 years before he died.

I never knew she had gone to a meeting.

She went twice and hated it.

She also told me that she almost killed my grandpa once.

I never knew why she hates to drive. She said she feels trapped in the car on long trips. Once my grandpa brought a bottle of booze with them while they were on a long road trip. She said he kept getting worse and worse. She said they stopped somewhere in the middle of nowhere and she thought *no one would know if I just ran over him and left.*

I haven't had a lot of time to talk to my grandma about these things. I have gone to her a couple times over the years to ask her advice when things were really bad. I remember those conversations very well.

Actually, I remember most of the things she has said to me. She doesn't open up a lot, so when she says something, I hold on to it. Now that her time is running out, I feel very sad. I keep thinking it is her codependency and my grandpa's alcoholism that have caused her cancer. *It eats at you.*

She said she preferred talking one-on-one with people as opposed to going to a big group and listening to everyone whine about their problems. I feel the same way. Sometimes I'm tired of listening to the same people week after week. It all seems so hopeless.

Maybe we should just all forget the addicts in our lives.

But how do you forget a child? That's what really kills me more than anyone else. When someone talks about losing a son or daughter to alcoholism or drugs, I *lose* it. That is one reason I really firmed my resolve for my own children.

I committed to attend six months of Al-Anon meetings while I was at "Family Week" at Betty Ford. I committed to *myself* that I would go for one year.

I do not think I will continue to go back on a weekly basis, as time is precious now that I am a single, working mother. But I haven't ruled it out on an as-needed basis.

The literature in particular has been very helpful to me. Several of the slogans are also great:

> "Life on life's terms."

> "Take what you like—leave the rest!"

> "Life is a package deal."

> "The three C's: You didn't Cause it, you can't Cure it, you can't Control it."

What I think was the most helpful to me was attending week after week and seeing patterns. It seems both the alcoholic (sober or not) and the co-dependent have marked personality traits.

I saw the same people come to the meeting every week. Some people got better, and others did not. Many people cried or complained every time about the same thing. The one thing I really noticed is that people who maintained a daily relationship with an addict never seemed to get all that better. The same frustrations kept surfacing.

It's easy to say *just leave the alcoholic in your life*. This is probably easier when it is your spouse—not your parent or your child.

I saw a lot of generational abuse of alcohol and drugs. My own thought after listening to a lot of this is that children model the behavior of their parents. I did see some interesting research about genetics while I was at Betty Ford. But overall, after being enmeshed in this for the last 7-8 years, I have to say that I think that this is learned behavior, mostly—or an attempt to soothe deep trauma.[4]

One thing I really liked about Al-Anon is that no one is supposed to tell you what to do. I think this really helps because often times when someone offers "helpful" advice, you want to do the *exact opposite*. I think listening to people week after week really helped me develop my own informed opinion about what would work best for me in my own life.

I am tired of focusing on my husband. I am ready to focus on the positive aspects of life. I believe I have learned more of what brought me into that relationship through Al-Anon, other reading, counseling and introspection.

---

[4] I highly recommend Gabor Maté's, *In the Realm of Hungry Ghosts: Close Encounters with Addiction*.

"All too often women believe it is a sign of commitment, an expression of love, to endure unkindness or cruelty, to forgive and forget. In actuality, when we love rightly we know that the healthy, loving response to cruelty and abuse
is putting ourselves out of harm's way."

-bell hooks

There are still far too many serious consequences to alcoholism and addiction for us to not begin to take this epidemic more seriously.

The problem I have with AA and Al-Anon is that they seem to work fine while you are working on them. But the minute you step away, you are back to being the same person.

I don't see that they are transformative in a lasting way.

It seems like something where you constantly have to attend meetings to reinforce behavior. And honestly, the never-ending slogans bug me.

The slogans in and of themselves are fine. There are a lot of truths to what is said. But my issue is that people seem to use these as band-aids when someone has a problem, instead of saying something more heartfelt and fitting to the occasion. It reminds me of Christians I know who become so indoctrinated that they never actually speak their own words anymore—they just quote Bible verses at you to address whatever your particular problem might be at the moment.

So while this may be an improvement for some people, I am just not fond of robots. I like people who are free thinkers. Perhaps that is just too ingrained in my personality—I take a little of this, and a little of that, and mix it all together and use what works.

I also don't think slogans go far enough to heal what is broken. When you create a mess—like the financial mess my husband has made for our family—you *fix* it. My husband hates it when I bring this up, but it is true.

It doesn't matter if you say you are sorry, or how many times you say you are sorry. "Sorry" doesn't mean anything when the offense is committed over and over again.

Randy Paush says that "proper apologies" have three parts:

> *What I did was wrong.*
> *I feel badly that I hurt you.*
> *How do I make you feel better?*
> -The Last Lecture

In my mind, you make someone feel better by amending what you did wrong. Sometimes this is not possible—like when you cheat on someone—other times, it *is*.

I think that's another downside of AA. People start to think that their behavior and their families are normal, and they are *not*. Most families don't behave like this. I think alcoholics should judge themselves by the standards that the rest of us have to live by.

My primary issue with AA and Al-Anon is that I think the programs should evolve. Nothing has really changed in more than 80 years, and we know a lot more about addiction and co-dependency now than we did when these programs were created.

I think there should be more integration between AA and Al-Anon —and I think we should be more integrated within society as a whole. There is still this secrecy around addiction that keeps it more dysfunctional.

"Patriarchy, hierarchy, and capitalism create, encourage, maintain, and perpetuate addiction and dependency. Patriarchy and hierarchy are based on domination and subordination, which result in fear. This fear is expressed by the dominators through control and violence, and in subordinated people through passivity and repression of anger. The external conflict of hierarchy between dominants and subordinates becomes internalized in individuals, creating personal inner chaos, anxiety and duality. To quell the inner conflict people resort to addictive substances and behavior."
-Charlotte Davis Kasl, PhD, *Many Roads, One Journey*

Sometimes I feel like Al-Anon is nothing more than a cult that brainwashes its members into staying in bad relationships. Obviously no one directly tells you to stay, but I certainly get that vibe from many, many people through their stories. And when I listen closely to those stories, the *staying* is concerning to me.

I have seen people get help through Al-Anon. I know it works for *some* people. But I mostly see people working *the program* instead of *living life*. Where is the *joy* in that? *Where is the living?*

"I didn't cause it, can't control it and can't cure it." That may be true for someone married to an alcoholic in terms of keeping the alcoholic's blame in check. But I think we know more about alcoholism than when that slogan was created. There are things that directly or indirectly "cause" or contribute to alcoholism— like sexual abuse, childhood trauma, consuming alcohol and drugs at a young age, and raising your children in dysfunctional (and/or alcoholic) homes. If you look at the statistics, these are all known factors.

If we know there *are* causes to alcoholism, why aren't we doing a better job of protecting our children? I really don't want to just sit things out and wait until my kids are teenagers so they can join Alateen. That is not a *solution* that I am OK with.

I think there are some good points to Al-Anon, but like the Bible, I don't think everything should just be accepted verbatim.

And I think it should be said that Al-Anon does not work for everyone. It is not the cure-all. To say, "It works when you work it," is victim-blaming in my mind. Some people—like my grandma —will *never* accept the program. She tried it, but it was not for her. That does not make her less of a person. She is actually one of the most amazing people I know. (And she has never once just spurted back a quick slogan to make me feel better—she talks like a real person, without slogans.)

If these programs were truly successful, we would already have generations without co-dependents and alcoholics. But I continually see families who are active in Al-Anon and AA where the cycle continues.

If alcoholism is a "disease," why aren't those of us who have been affected so tremendously not demanding better solutions?

"The past is not a burden; it is a scaffold, which brought us to this day. We are free to be whom we are—to create our own life out of our past and out of the present. We are our ancestors. When we can heal ourselves, we also heal our ancestors, our grandmothers, our grandfathers and our children.
When we heal ourselves, we heal Mother Earth."

-Grandmother Rita Pitka Blumenstein

I have been reflecting a lot on my first marriage, and all that has transpired since then. I came from a sheltered conservative Christian background and I married very young to a Lebanese Shiite Muslim. I often wonder if that alone didn't ruin us. But there were a lot of other obstacles as well.

In any case, I now count Hussein as one of my dearest friends. His wife is also extremely close to me and I adore his children. I know that not everyone chooses to remain close to their ex—especially when there are no children involved. But I feel that Hussein will forever remain a part of me, and that I owe him so much for who I have become.

Last night, I joined his family at their home for dinner. I brought a cake that my daughter and I made for his wife. She recently had her appendix out. While she was sitting in the hospital she said she was craving this cake that I make, and asked me if I would make her one.

So we decided to cook Lebanese food together, which is something we both enjoy. We decided earlier this year that we both cook better together than apart. I think part of it is that we just enjoy each other's company so much.

So I arrived late in the afternoon with my kids and we let them play, while we opened a bottle of wine and started cooking and talking about life. Hussein came in and out of the room, and joined us later for the meal.

We talked about our marriages, our in-laws and our children.

They said that they both had noticed when they saw me last week that I have been happier and light-hearted lately than I have been for a while. I told them that I had decided that no matter what, I am going to laugh and be happy. Whether things work out or they don't—or I have money, or anything else—I have to get through my days, and I may as well laugh.

We talked about how when you have children with someone, you are forever bound to that person whether you are married or not —so you may as well make the most of it and try to get along.

One thing that I have always wondered about is whether I could have made my first marriage work, if I had given it some time. I don't have regrets over that now. It is what it is, and I don't think things could have worked out more beautifully than they have. But it does make me approach my current marriage differently than someone else might. I think I have, perhaps, tried too hard to make this second marriage work.

"After all, when it comes to connection and dependence, 'equality' is a quandary: we might well hear the word 'dependence' and immediately think 'drugs', 'co-dependency in addiction' or 'welfare'. And the reason? The neoliberal hand has been busy turning a necessary and inevitable part of the human condition into a frailty, a flaw or a felony. Dependence is something which renders us somehow lacking as a citizen: unequal. Those of us at the coalface of care know that superficial ideas of equality marginalise carers because if we are busy seeing to the needy, the powers that be can ignore our needs and rights. They can pathologise us into 'dependants' in a language which usually reserves such labels for miscreants, addicts or otherwise 'pathetic people' our society can 'do without'. Dependency has been thoroughly stigmatised."

-Vanessa Olorenshaw

I am home today for the second day—trying to work and take care of two sick kids. Going back to work with young children seems almost impossible to me these days. Now that both kids are in different schools, there is always at least one day a week when one or both is either sick or off school. I can already see the effect it has on my work, which is slow to begin with.

The mortgage industry is definitely not what it used to be. I don't see myself making a good income there anymore without 1) gauging people and going against my own principles, and 2) working ungodly hours and ditching my kids somewhere when they are sick or unable to go to school. And even if I was willing to compromise on either or both of those things, it still is not going to provide the income that it used to.

A lot of my friends in the industry are getting out altogether, or already have. In my state, we went from 15,000 mortgage originators to 5,000. I think that will continue to go down—and one could say that I could reap the benefits. But there are also so few people who qualify for loans these days that I think more people should probably get out. Half the time I start a loan only to find out that I can't do it for some reason halfway through the process (or worse yet, at the end). Usually this is because the value of the home has dropped too far down.

I am completely commission-based, so if the loan does not fund, I do not get paid for any of my work.

I am growing tired of all the new regulations. What keeps me in is the flexibility and my clients.

That said, I still need to be able to make a living.

I have been thinking about this a lot lately, and trying to rack my brain for any other ideas. The job market is very bad in Oregon— one of the worst in the nation. But there has to be *something.*

I wish I could just raise my kids and not worry. But money is a constant concern.

I wish our society placed more value on raising children well. I don't think there is anything more crucial than that. But it seems to be a luxury mostly reserved for the wealthy. Now that I have refused to play by my husband's rules, our children apparently no longer deserve that comfort.

We have an enormous budget to tackle every month—and once you have established that, you can't very well go back on most of your commitments. I have cut down, and cut down, and cut down —but there is still a lot to pay every month. If I could go back and do it over again, I would have been more involved in our budget from the get-go.

> "You have to learn to get up from the table when love
> is no longer being served."
>
> -Nina Simone

I feel sad and alone—and angry. I feel trapped. I feel stuck. I feel broke.

In my being, I know that I need to get out of this marriage. But the bottom line is, I don't know how we will manage financially. Even if we were to walk away from our home and our debt, it would still be a struggle.

There's a woman in my office who is like a second mother to me. She came in and practically begged me the other day to get out of my marriage. She told me about how she stayed with her husband until her kids were in their twenties and it only got worse with time. She emailed me her attorney's name and contacted him to let him know I'd be calling and asked if he'd meet with me for free. She said I deserve to be happy and safe.

However, I can't seem to find an attorney who will work with me without a huge retainer. Once I meet with them, it seems my case will be very expensive to defend.

I don't know how to balance my needs with those of my children. I worry about them so much. I don't think this family is healthy for them either, but then I think, if we can't *live*, what's the point?

My friend Bill said I'd be happy when I started to make decisions that are good for *me*.

I worry that if I don't get out soon, this marriage will destroy me.

> "This is a good sign, having a broken heart.
> It means we have tried for something."
> -Elizabeth Gilbert

My daughter fell asleep on the way to school this morning, so I turned around and went home after we dropped my son off. Turns out that was a good choice. She obviously does not feel well. We are spending a quiet day together.

My first husband and his wife just came back from a long trip to Lebanon. Her parents had come to my office yesterday and told me they were back, so I decided to visit them.

It sounds like they had a wonderful trip. I wish I had been able to go with them. Yesterday, her parents offered to take me, and today she invited me to come with her this summer.

How I miss Lebanon.

Americans seem to wonder why the Lebanese and the Palestinians fight so hard for their land. If they had been there, they would understand.

It is beautiful in Lebanon. And the people are the best of the best. There is no place more hospitable, or filled with love and laughter. I have never seen children so happy and well behaved. They are free to run around the village without care, because everyone watches out for everyone else. The high school kids are smarter than most college graduates I know. Most people speak Arabic, French and English, and the children study psychology, literature, mathematics in all three languages, which is different than just taking a French or English class.

The people of Lebanon are very present—perhaps because they have lost so much. When I visited in 1995, Israel was still bombing nearby. My first husband is from a small village in the South of Lebanon. I remember being scared many times, but after a while, you get used to it. There is no place I have enjoyed traveling to more than Lebanon. It touched my soul.

Since I met my second husband, I have essentially stopped traveling—at least abroad. I really want to change that.

I enjoyed hearing all the stories of the people I love back in Lebanon. My sister-in-law just lost her husband. I remember them well from my visit there. He had a brain tumor then. It is amazing, really, that he made it this long.

We talked about the traditions of death in Lebanon. I remember going to a funeral while I was there. A teen boy was killed by an Israeli soldier during my stay. Nearly everyone from all surrounding villages stopped what they were doing and drove to his village for the funeral. There must have been thousands of people there. I will never forget the sound of the women wailing —screaming really—at the top of their lungs, with all of their hearts and souls.

I think I understand those screams even more now that I have my own children. The grief is unimaginable.

But I think that wailing is good for the soul. In America, death is often skipped over. In Lebanon, the family is in mourning for 40 days. The widow is never left alone. There are usually about 10 people with her at all times, to care for her needs and give her company. Every day, for a period of 40 days, the entire family visits the graveside.

I think that is beautiful. Hussein's wife told me, "One of the things I like most about our culture is that we make everyone feel so special." I think she really nailed it on the head.

Yesterday, her parents visited me at my office and brought donuts and special Lebanese pastries. My entire office was thrilled.

My daughter's namesake still lives in the South of Lebanon. She is one of Hussein's many aunts. I remember being instantly taken with her. She is everything I wanted my daughter to be—smart and always laughing—with a *very* strong sense of herself. Her spirit was beautiful and amazing.

I decided when I met her that I would name my daughter after her —even though I was nowhere close to having kids then. I was still in college and wanted to finish my degree first. The Masters degree was one of several things that killed our marriage—but primarily, it was my youth. In retrospect, I don't think anyone should marry before the age of 30.

Hussein handled our divorce with so much grace. One of the best gifts that he ever gave to me, when I was feeling guilty was to tell me, "Despite everything, you are still the best person I have ever known." I will never forget those words, and he will never know how much they meant to me coming from him. When I am feeling low, I still can hear him telling me that, and it still helps tremendously.

I sent pictures of my daughter to show the family and especially her namesake. She was very pleased with them and sent my daughter back a dress. On Saturday we will go visit them. It sounds like they brought back many gifts, which is a tradition. I am looking forward to seeing their entire family. I miss all of them. They will always be my family.

Within days of arriving in Lebanon, Hussein's grandma sat me on her lap and told me, "I love you just as much as I love Hussein. You are now a daughter to me." All of his family treated me that way.

"Women who join together with each other to deny the male god who cursed their sex and to reject his demands for obedience, praise, service and money automatically free themselves from one of the most potent psychological traps men ever set for them! Without god to tell them that they must serve and obey abusive husbands, their shackles turn to sand—and they can step away from what seemed a prison."

-Barbara G. Walker

I have been spending a lot of time thinking about why Al-Anon does not "work" for me. I don't mean that it's a bad program, or that it does not have merit, but I don't think it's a cure-all.

I have been thinking that Al-Anon is a very American program, and although I am an American, I tend not to think like one.

I rarely see anyone but Americans in my meetings. There are occasionally some British people and one Russian woman. Obviously all societies have addicts, so I am wondering what other cultures do. I know that Al-Anon and AA have groups everywhere, but I don't believe either program is as prevalent in any other culture.

I also have been thinking a great deal about religion lately. While Al-Anon is supposed to be non-affiliated, it seems very Christian to me. It does not mesh philosophically with what I believe as a Muslim. I suppose I can somewhat relate to it from my Christian upbringing, but I have yet to see another Muslim in any Al-Anon meeting. (Although I do have one Muslim friend online who attends Al-Anon meetings abroad.)

I talked recently with a Mormon who had tried Al-Anon and she felt similarly. I also talked to another friend who does not like Al-Anon at all because she is an atheist and it is "too Christian" for her. We talked about another friend who was Jewish who had similar sentiments.

I think the similarities that I see between these other religions is that they tend to be very family-oriented. Whereas Westernized Christianity encourages forgiveness and more of a personal relationship with Jesus, these other groups tend to emphasize responsibility to the group.

A Muslim man who does not take care of his family because of alcoholism would be shunned. This might not be ideal for the alcoholic, but I sure don't know many Muslim alcoholics. What is better for the family and the community as a *whole* is what is primary. If someone strays from that, they are taken aside and held to account. If they still cannot behave, the group would shun them. Thus, you do not often see this behavior.

Conversely, I would also argue that addiction is at least partially caused by a *lack* of community. As Johann Harri says, "The opposite of addiction is not sobriety. The opposite of addiction is connection."

Reading authors like Gabor Maté and David Sheff has given me more compassion for addicts. I strongly believe that our individualistic society, which does not value family—and especially the cardinal role that mothers play in bringing up healthy children—has a tremendous role in the tragic increase in addiction. I believe when we value individual and communal well-being over money, we will see a different world.

That said, I think we often gloss over the consequences of the addict's behavior on their immediate family. In fact, we sometimes blame the co-dependent almost equally.

I do not think we would ask someone in a concentration camp what *their part in it* was.

I find the conditions of living in an alcoholic home to be completely inhumane. I think Al-Anon sometimes encourages us (perhaps inadvertently) to stay in bad situations and "look at our part" instead of getting out.

I remember when I was at a Betty Ford workshop for married couples listening to many stories that made my skin crawl. The facilitators were telling us that we had basically equal responsibility in the relationship. My husband likes to pull this out during an argument, but I have never believed this.

In her book, *The Verbally Abusive Relationship*, Patricia Evans explains that for a therapist to even *suggest* this to an abused woman, is to abuse them over again.

One woman was with an alcoholic who treated her horribly and cheated on her. To this day, I still cannot see her "equal" part in this. She was a very kind woman. Every time her husband spoke, I could not believe the justifications that were coming out of his mouth for his continually poor behavior. If I could go back, I would tell all of those women to *get the hell out of the relationship*—and *then* look at their part, if they had any.

Al-Anon often seems rather cult-like to me in that (especially the online community) is always trying to convince you how well it works. To me, if it worked that well, we would not hear about the continual problems stemming from the alcoholic. One of the things that attracted me to Islam is that no one ever tried to recruit me. I just watched people who I thought were beautiful inside and wanted to learn more.

I also find it strange when people in "recovery" encourage you to only talk to other people in "recovery" and insinuate that everyone else is somehow emotionally unhealthy. I understand that people in the program have been through similar situations, but most of the people I meet in the program seem to have significantly more problems than people outside of the program.

It seems to me that if you want to find answers in your life, you should look to people who are living in healthy situations. I have seen several people who seem sage-like in Al-Anon, but the proportion of healthy people outside of Al-Anon and AA seems much greater to me.

I find it offensive when people in Al-Anon think that their method is the only one that works. It may be the most widespread program, but I think saying that it works for all people is like saying Christianity is the only "true" religion. My perspective on religion is that God/dess created many types of people and hence there is a belief system out there that works for everyone. (Atheism *is* also a belief system in my book.)

"God as we understand HIM" also underscores the patriarchy inherent in nearly all the world religions as they are practiced. I do not believe any organization that supports patriarchal thinking can be good for women as a whole.

Al-Anon and AA are one option—but I have come to realize that there are many, many more.[5] One thing I will say from my experience of attending meetings is they do help to normalize what you are feeling. But after a while, you are just in the same swirl, with the same people, doing the same things over and over again. Personally, I needed to get out of that and start engaging in more meaningful activities. Otherwise, I think I would still be in that same cycle.

When you fill your life up with good things, there is very little time for the bad. For a long time, I was too consumed with the bad to even consider doing something positive. Even if I did have something fun planned, I would often cancel it. Today, even if I feel bad about something, I try very hard to keep my plans, and I usually end up having a great time.

---

[5] See the Suggested Reading section at the end of this book.

The two things that have helped me the *most* with my recovery are feminism and volunteering.

Volunteering is probably an obvious thing. When you help others, you forget about your own problems. There were many years where I was so enmeshed in my own life that I didn't even consider volunteering. I wish I had done this earlier. It would have taken me out of my own head. It also would have put me in touch with more positive-minded people instead of isolating myself.

In terms of feminism, taking Women's Studies in college was eye-opening. I think that was one of the biggest periods of growth in my life. Feminism is important because we are not socialized as girls to see our worth. It is especially valuable for those of us who are co-dependents because feminism is one of the only things that can *truly* empower us as women.

"The truth about our childhood is something we cannot, and should not, forgo, either as individuals or as a society. One of the reasons is that behind the wall we erect to protect ourselves from the history of our childhood still stands the neglected child we once were, the child that was once abandoned and betrayed. She waits for us to summon the courage to hear her voice. She wants to be protected and understood, and she wants us to free her from her isolation, loneliness, and speechlessness. But this child who has waited so long for our attention not only has needs to be fulfilled. She also has a gift for us, a gift that we desperately need if we truly want to live, a gift that cannot be purchased and that the child in us alone can bestow. It is the gift of truth, which can free us from the prison of destructive opinions and conventional lies. Ultimately, it is the gift of security, which our rediscovered integrity will give us. The child only waits for us to be ready to approach her, and then, together, we will tear down the walls."

-Alice Miller, *Breaking Down the Wall of Silence*

The one thing I did get from doing my fourth step in Al-Anon was a realization about my trust level in God.

I consider myself a spiritual person, but I realized that I do not really trust God to take care of me. I know that goes back to my childhood.

I have depended too much on my husband to *take care of me*. I wish I had taken back the reigns to my life sooner. I think what they say about *turning the alcoholic into our god* was true for me.

Life was often unpredictable and scary for me. I would stay up all night worrying about what *he* would do instead of praying to God for guidance and help. I can remember very few times when I prayed and asked God for *help*. The Serenity Prayer has always worked for me, but I often get out of the habit of using it.

Having children was very healing for me. I went to a therapist during my entire pregnancy with my son, and got a lot of issues resolved from childhood. Raising children gave me tremendous grace toward my own parents. I realize now how hard they worked and appreciate their many sacrifices.

I think both of my parents truly did the best they could throughout my childhood (sometimes much more).

I had some resentment toward my mother prior to having my daughter that I have since resolved. The conclusion that I have come to is that my parents married way too young—and, once divorced, remarried too soon.

After being a single mom, I can understand now why they both remarried again so quickly. It is very, very hard to suddenly do everything (well) on your own. Every day, I feel I have failed my children on some level. I don't believe that raising children is a one-person job.

I do not *blame* my parents anymore. I do not think I would make the same choices though.

My relationship with both my stepparents was difficult. I do not speak to either stepparent anymore, and I have no desire to. Any abuse I suffered as a child was at the hands of a stepparent. I used to blame my parents for not protecting me better, but I now know that abusive people conduct their abuse in secret. Silence is their weapon.

I used to dream as a child that my parents would get back together, but as an adult I see that they were never right for each other. I would not have wanted my parents to stay together unhappily for my sake. I hope to make good choices from these reflections so that my children will have a different experience.

I made the decision long ago that I did not want to have

stepparents for my children. I think that being a stepparent is a nearly impossible job. I do have empathy now for both of my stepparents and I have forgiven them. But I am also not in a place now where I want to have contact with either of them.

I realized the other day that I have been very closed-minded about all of this. Even my father-in-law told me several times when things were very bad with my husband that I should remarry and find a nice stepfather for the kids. I told him emphatically that I did *not* want to do that.

I think I have been living in fear about all the what-ifs that could happen with my kids. I think that is one reason I have tried so hard to protect my children and control the outcomes of who can be around them and in what regard. I have this gnawing fear about letting anyone who could possibly hurt my children around them. I know from experience, that unkind words hurt long after they are said.

I had the feeling growing up that if I became a *good enough* Christian, that God would protect me. I went to church nearly every day and was always reading my Bible and praying. I thought that the better person or Christian I was, the more God would favor me.

That did not happen. After starting a Religion major in college, I hit a wall with my faith. I could not believe *at all*. I cried and prayed about it, but I could not believe anymore. I became an atheist for a time.

It was not until I met my first husband that I regained any spirituality.

As life progressed, I realized that I was also free to go back to some of my Christian beliefs and services. I do not have to be in a "Muslim" or "Atheist" box. I began to feel very good about my spirituality as a thinking and questioning person. I did not feel trapped and I did not have that fear about *going to hell* that I did growing up.

Children have an innocence about them that is so beautiful. There is no fear in their love or their belief. As life goes on, sometimes this innocence is tainted and we lose our faith. Or we believe that we have to be "just so" for God to love us—or even for us to love ourselves.

What I like about my current beliefs is that I don't "try" to be a Christian or a Muslim or anything. I just *am*. And that is good enough.

While I think I have come a long way in my spiritual journey, I have never regained that complete trust in God that I had when I was a little kid.

"I've learned that people will forget what you said, people will forget what you did, but people will never forget how you made them feel."

-Maya Angelou

For some reason, I thought back to "Family Week" at Betty Ford today and an image has been stuck in my head.

There was a beautiful and kind woman there with me, and I grew to love her almost instantly. We still keep in touch, and she is very dear to my heart.

At one point during the week, we were supposed to confront the addict in our lives and express the pain they had caused us. Her husband was not there, so she addressed someone else, or maybe it was a chair—my memory fails me. Her face was so mesmerizing in that moment that I did not really notice anything else.

I do not remember most of the things she said, but I do remember how real and raw her pain felt. I remember thinking, *here is this beautiful, amazing, compassionate woman*—and she did not deserve *any* of this.

I do not remember my moment or what was said to my husband.

At that point, I think I skipped over a lot of things because I don't like being under pressure or in the spotlight. In some ways, I think it would have been better if he had not been there because I think I tried to spare a lot of his feelings and humiliation instead of getting rid of everything in my heart.

"The key to our power is feeling. When we fearlessly own the full spectrum of our emotions, we begin to own the truth of who we are. Sometimes to discover this, we have to descent to our depths to repair old wounds or unearth old desires. But out of the old pieces and the new we form a new creation—our lives. The results of such work are always positive even if some of the steps we take to achieve them cause pain. But that pain is short-term. The pain of never owning our full, rich, authentic selves lasts forever."

-Karen Andes, *A Woman's Book of Power*

I have been thinking about my birthday, which is in a few weeks. I will be turning 35. My husband mentioned that he would like to take me out to dinner with the kids. I said I wasn't sure because it seems like we only argue now when we spend time together. I don't want to spend my birthday fighting.

I was thinking back to his 37th birthday, the year after he relapsed. We were separated but had decided to go to dinner as a family.

During dinner, my son asked in his little 5-year-old voice, *Daddy, why are you an alcoholic?*

There was a long awkward pause. My husband's face looked crushed. I can't remember what we said but I remember it did not seem adequate.

I remember my husband later telling me that he cried on the way home. I thought of all this and felt extremely sad. I don't know if he *chose* to relapse. I tend to think that because I can't understand taking a drink after three years of sobriety. In that moment at least, I know that he felt remorse—which is something I rarely see from him.

I think the hardest thing for me to accept in all of this is that my husband has rarely appeared to be sorry for his actions. And his actions have caused all of us a lot of pain.

People make mistakes. I accept that. But repeat offenses are hard to accept.

I am sad that addiction has taken over his family. I have often thought that he was pretty much destined to be an addict in that family. I had always hoped things would get better with him.

But wishing does not make it so.

> "Women have to understand that regardless of who does not want us we have to want ourselves. Self-love is the first and hardest rule to stick by. Women need to not abandon themselves in their quest for bliss and love. You can love yourself spiritually, physically, in almost any way anybody else can."
>
> -Alice Walker

Last night, my husband read my blog again and sent me a 7-point response, defending himself. It is clear that we both have *completely different* versions of reality. My husband does not even pretend to be his nice-guy persona anymore around other people. Sometimes I think it was hard for people to envision the things that he said to me. That's no longer the case.

A friend told me the other day that when he called me a *cunt*, that's when it would have been over for her. It's funny how you try to remove these things from your mind, but when you finally tell people what has happened—and they remind you of them— you are not able to create your own (better) reality anymore. Hearing her say it made me realize how awful things have been.

You don't expect to ever have to worry about contracting HIV or STD's anymore when you get married. At least I didn't. Maybe I was naive.

However, I think I felt like my husband was still in the process of making amends to me and never would go "there."

I remember a friend of mine who went through a very similar situation, with an alcoholic husband and 4 children. After getting through recovery with him, she then found out her husband was cheating on her. My husband said at the time he thought that was horrible.

I have known for some time that my husband cheated on me

during our marriage. I thought it was only once and with one woman. I assumed he would have at least given me the courtesy of using a condom.

I am done pretending that it wasn't as bad or that he did it while we were separated. I know that was not the case. I am done letting my husband think he has gotten away with something.

One of the most humiliating experiences of my life was having to go in to my doctor and ask for an HIV test while I was still breastfeeding. After asking me why—and telling him about the cocaine in the home—he asked me if my husband was sleeping with prostitutes. He suggested I get fully tested for everything. Luckily, nothing came up but it scared the hell out of me. And I have yet to get even an acknowledgment from my husband, yet alone an apology.

Yesterday, my husband asked me when the last time I tried to make *him* feel good was. I gave him two recent examples. The first was when I tried to make him feel better about our daughter not wanting to go with him. The second was late last week when I made tostados. I know he likes them and I let him take all the leftovers, despite the fact that we barely have money for groceries right now.

He was not able to acknowledge either thing. I told him I have always been nice to him and done things to make him feel better, but he has taken me for granted.

I told him it never mattered how nice I was to you—you still ended up with your dick inside someone else.

He said *I left him*. That I had left him a *long time ago*.

I told him to stop lying. He seems to forget that I found a $500 hotel bill in town that he couldn't explain. I told him that I knew the truth, and have always known it on some level.

My husband seems to think that his behaviors have some justification. But there is no justification for cheating on your wife. He feels that I *didn't take care of him*. Even if that *were* true, it does not make it right.

I seem to remember when his mother died *that* was an excuse to start drinking again. But I was there for him then. I ran out of the vet's office the second he called, mid-appointment and rushed out to be with him. I called his dad and said I was worried that this would cause him to relapse. I did everything in my power to make sure he had adequate support.

But in the end, it was his choice to drink again. It was his choice to be with other women. He never told me then that he felt neglected. It is only now that everything is out in the open that he tries to blame me for *his* actions.

It's not going to fly. I will not take responsibility for his cheating. He needs to take responsibility for himself. He cannot blame me, he cannot blame his parents, and he cannot blame his friends. He needs to look at himself.

I am done trying to make him feel better.

"Growth involves breaking and healing. And risking a new vision."
-Louise M. Wisechild, *The Obsidian Mirror*

For a long time, I have held on to this idea of being married and raising our kids together. But as my counselor always told me, I was holding onto a dream of how I *wanted* things to be and not the reality of how things *are* with my husband.

Our society puts so much emphasis on being a part of a relationship—especially when you have children. I think I have really bought into that. Single mothers are second class citizens in so many ways.

Mothers and wives also seem to be wary of a single attractive woman. Many of my male friends keep telling me, "you just need to put on about 20 pounds, and then all the wives will feel comfortable around you."

I am not interested in being with anyone's husband. I am not really interested in being with *any* man.

I think it is sad that fear makes us do so many things. Tony Robbins says most people will do "more to avoid pain than to obtain pleasure."

I'd rather be a whole person than a half of a dysfunctional relationship.

"A slut is someone, usually a woman, who's stepped outside of the very narrow lane that good girls are supposed to stay within. Sluts are loud. We're messy. We don't behave. In fact, the original definition of "slut" meant "untidy woman." But since we live in a world that relies on women to be tidy in all ways, to be quiet and obedient and agreeable and available (but never aggressive), those of us who color outside of the lines get called sluts.
And that word is meant to keep us in line."

-Jaclyn Friedman

My son's birthday was ruined by my husband, with my son ending up in tears.

My husband decided to bring up a bunch of stuff at my son's birthday dinner about what he imagined my sexual life to be.

I only wish I was having as much sex as he supposes.

I am a sexual woman. I always have been. I do not have guilt or shame around that.

I never cheated on my husband while we were together. He did.

But because I am a woman there is some bullshit double standard.

And I don't buy into that.

But I also don't think that it is appropriate for him to bring up what he "thinks" I have done—after our relationship is over—in front of our three and seven-year-old children.

I have never told my son what my husband did with other women. Why would I?

It has nothing to do with him.

Even if I were a "whore," I don't believe that would make me less of a person.

I absolutely do not believe that.

We as woman have intrinsic worth, above and beyond what society labels us as. Jesus himself hung out with prostitutes, which is something Christians seem to forget.

There is nothing wrong with our sexuality. Nothing. God Herself created it.

I will not let my son suffer. Perhaps this was a lesson learned—and better for him to learn it now. *Women are women*. They are not whores or sluts. Women are not less than any man for having the same sexuality that men are free to express without question or remark.

I took my son aside, held him tight, and told him, "You know who I am. Never forget that."

Later, my son told my daughter and me, "What daddy called you is something no one should call anyone."

I received another 100 text messages from my husband the following day. Most of them consisting of calling me a "tramp," a "whore," or something along those lines.

I spent most of my life living as a "good girl." I did all the things I was supposed to do. This did not protect me from being called a *cunt, bitch, whore, slut, tramp* or whatever else when I was not doing whatever a certain man in my life thought I *should* be doing.

"All who seek to know Me, know this... All your seeking and yearning will be in vain unless you understand the Mystery that if what you seek is not found within, you will never find it without. For behold, I have been with you from the beginning, and I will gather you to my breast at the end."

-Doreen Valiente, from "Charge of the Goddess"

I feel very raw. I feel like I am suffocating underneath the weight of a giant piano squishing my chest.

My husband told me it hurt him to hear me cry like this—but he will never understand that he caused my pain.

I realized that there are a lot of things I could do right now to numb myself—whether it be working hard or starting to date. But I really need to deal with all of this before I move on to anything else.

I need to heal.

"To step outside of patriarchal thought means overcoming the deep-seated resistance within ourselves toward accepting ourselves and our knowledge as valid. It means getting rid of the great men in our heads and substituting them for ourselves, our sisters, our anonymous foremothers."

-Gerda Lerner, *The Creation of Patriarchy*

Today is my husband's birthday. We had a busy day planned but agreed that he would come and get the kids for a few hours. He wanted to take them to lunch and then to see his parents.

My daughter had been dreading this all day. When my husband arrived, he tried to force the issue.

I told him my grandmother had a suggestion.

Your daughter is still very young. Forcing her at this age will only make things worse. Take it slow—let her work into it. She's still very young to go with him alone—when she is ready, she will want to. Right now, if she doesn't want to go, just take the boy.

I thought this made a lot of sense. My grandmother had 5 kids and many grandchildren. I respect her.

But for an hour, my husband continued to push my daughter, taking her several times anyway from me, with her kicking and screaming.

I tried to speak reasonably with him. He doesn't seem to understand. He just wanted to keep debating it.

He had also arrived late, so by then it was 2 PM and none of us had eaten lunch. I told him that (in and of itself) did not work well for any of us.

Our son had gotten in the car, but after 15 minutes of that, he ran out and stood by my daughter and I. He had decided that he did not want to go either.

I felt sorry for my husband. It was his birthday. I know his dad will give him hell, which will probably put more pressure on him. But I do not believe forcing the kids to go with him is good for anyone.

He still believes it is—and called me afterwards to continue the argument. I told him I'd like to see our son's counselor together and get her professional opinion. He agreed to go, but continued to badger me.

I told him I had to go.

My life continues to get better and better as I focus on other things. But these arguments are very draining. I still have a lot to do for a fundraiser today, but quite honestly, I don't feel like doing a damned thing.

Divorcing Everything

"At any rate, as my lawyer explained, the law then was the same
as the law today; the courts would surely award me a reasonable
amount of the father's income as child support, but the courts
would also insist that they could not enforce their own decree.
In other words, according to the law, what a father owes to his
child is not serious compared to what a man owes
to the bank for a car, or a vacation."

-June Jordan

My husband just left and I am once again disappointed. It seems
there will be no easy way out of this. His dad paid a $5,000
retainer for his divorce attorney. *So much for coming to an
amicable agreement on our own.*

It amazes me that there is no money to pay bills or take care of
the majority of the needs of our children—including counseling
for our son or even getting his cavities filled—but there is money
for an attorney, which will surely cost more than $5,000. If that is
not abuse and neglect, I don't know what is.

Apparently it is more important for my husband and his father to
protect their money than to take care of these kids.

I had another mostly sleepless night last night. I am back to
listening to my New Age tapes—Louise Hay right now. I started
doing some affirmations and meditations to help me sleep. I
realized last night how hard it has become—my mind wanders
almost immediately.

I think I have really begun to hate myself. I thought I just hated
what my life (for the most part) has become and the actions of my

husband and his family. But it became apparent last night that this negativity has transferred to me too.

I think it's hard for me to forgive now because I went through all this before when my husband went to rehab the first time. I wasn't sure I should continue in the relationship. But I decided it was better for my son and I worked on myself while he was at rehab for two months.

I felt at that time, that all was forgiven. I did not bring up the past. We had a few good years together—including the birth of our daughter, which was a very joyous time for me.

But then, he relapsed—and now I almost feel foolish for not believing that he would. It seems now it would have been easier to move on at the time of the first rehab.

Now I am two kids in and many more years. I don't want to keep feeling this way.

"Children need two things: roots and wings."

-Chinese Proverb

I have begun the process of selling my wedding rings. This has been a difficult decision for me and one I did not take lightly.

My husband proposed on Lake Washington four and a half years ago. We were celebrating our three-year anniversary together. On the way up from Oregon, I remember asking him if he was *ever* going to marry me. We already had a son and he was just about to celebrate one year of sobriety.

Early in my relationship with my husband, I became pregnant. When we met, I was in my mid-twenties and still having a good time myself. It was quickly apparent that he had a drinking problem when I stopped drinking with news of the pregnancy. I wrote my future father-in-law a letter, shocked with my discovery. He told me I wasn't telling him anything he didn't already know.

In any case, we did stay together through most of that time and I was thrilled when he became sober about a year after our son was born.

The night before he proposed, we watched some corny wedding movie and I started crying about us never getting married. Little did I know that the next day he had rented this beautiful old restored wooden sailboat for us with a picnic lunch and champagne for me. He got on one knee and produced a ring with three diamonds, (past-present-future) totaling about 2.5 carats. It was much bigger than I had ever expected. It was the perfect proposal in every way, but it was not an indicator of the life to come for us.

On our wedding day he produced another surprise: an eternity band consisting of another four carats of sparkling diamonds. The two rings together were stunning. We had a perfect Country Club wedding. Everything went on without a hitch. Even my father-in-law was on good behavior. But all the happiness and pretty things surrounding that occasion were in no way indicative of the life we would have together later.

For many years those rings have been sort of a security blanket for me. But I think big diamonds and beautiful jewelry can also mask other things. For a long time, everyone thought my husband was a "good guy" because he gave me fancy things. The over-the-top-ness of it all really covered up a lot of other BS. Being a good partner to someone has nothing to do with the gifts that you give them. Gifts are a nice perk, but they shouldn't overshadow or compensate for everything else.

It was nice to hear a friend tell me several weeks ago, "Hey, it's good to see you without your rings on." I think she saw it as a sign of my own inner strength.

It's easy to let diamonds and designer bags tell people "who we are." They are an instant status boost. But when it comes down to it, those things are really not who I am.

But part of me is still sad to see the rings go. I have sold most of the expensive gifts from my husband off these last years to pay bills, but the rings were one thing I held on to.

The bottom line is that I need the money now to feed my kids. So I have to sell the rings.

"If you stick a knife in my back nine inches and pull it out six inches, that's not progress. If you pull it all the way out, that's not progress. The progress comes from healing the wound that the blow made. They haven't even begun to pull the knife out. They won't even admit the knife is there."

-Malcolm X

My husband and I went back and forth yesterday about the temporary divorce agreement, but were never able to agree on anything. I told him I would not budge about letting the kids spend the night with him and that was non-negotiable.

I found out late this afternoon that I needed to be in court tomorrow. I still have no attorney. I cannot afford one.

I think I now know why my husband was playing the "*I want to work things out*" game. If I had sold my rings earlier, I would have had the money to pay for at least some legal representation.

In any case, the kids and I had agreed to go to my first husband's house for dinner last night and I'm glad we did. His wife made a very hearty Lebanese meal and I left well fortified in mind, body and spirit.

I was able to see some of their pictures from their recent trip to Lebanon and she gave me copies of my favorite ones. It meant so much to me because my old photo album was stolen years ago and I have very few pictures of my former father-in-law, who I adore.

I stashed the pictures in my purse and took them to court with me today for good luck. I also wore the ring his sister bought for me when I went to Lebanon. It is traditional to buy the bride gold. In times of financial hardship, the woman has her gold to sell, so it is considered a sort of financial security. (And gold is very easy to buy and sell in Lebanon.) I have never been able to bring myself to sell the gold from Hussein's family. It is very sentimental to me. I know that was money that did not come easy for them. I remember going with them to pick out what I liked and feeling very guilty about their purchases. They were gifts that involved sacrifice.

That said, I wish I had more of a Lebanese attitude toward my jewelry. I am extremely sentimental. It has always been hard for me to let go.

It amazes me that Hussein came to the United States with no money or English skills. When I met him, he worked at Dunkin Donuts full-time (we actually met there) and worked two other menial jobs. He never took any money from his family— everything he has is from his own two hands.

He started college and several businesses while we were married. While he is not "rich," I consider him a complete success. His wife and children want for nothing.

Sometimes I think coming from a wealthy family is much more of a hindrance than coming from nothing. When you make it on your own, you appreciate it.

While I was visiting with Hussein's wife, I noticed I had a missed call from my dad. I knew he was away on business so I figured it was urgent. I checked my message and it was vague, asking me to call him right away.

As it turns out, his mother is not doing well. Her heart is very bad.

We all rushed over.

She told me she was hungry for some fried chicken and that I am the only person who can make it the way she likes it. I have my great-grandmother's recipe that she taught me to make as a teenager. I really didn't master it until a few years ago. You'd think fried chicken would be easy, but it's really an art.

We stopped on the way home at two different markets to find the kind of chicken she likes. I soaked it in buttermilk overnight and woke up at 5:30 to fry it all. I figured I would make some bacon for my kids while I was up—and made some for Nano because she had said a few weeks ago she missed that too.

My son woke up with a double ear infection. I decided he needed to go to the doctor for antibiotics. I made him a 10 AM appointment. It was nice to get a hug from our pediatrician; he's been a stable force in my life since I was born. My mom joined us at the visit to take my son so I could make it to work and court.

Prior to that, we visited Nano. She was really thrilled with the fried chicken—and I made her some coffee and toast to go with her bacon for breakfast.

I'm really glad we got that visit in. Last night was very difficult with both children there. My daughter was very restless and unruly. I felt like we got a good visit in this morning. I don't know how much time she has left, so today meant a lot to me.

We had asked her to come home with us last night but she wanted to stay in her own bed. I hope that Nano realizes how much we all love her and never feels alone in her death.

I really got upset with my husband last night around all of this. I feel like because of his relapse I have not been able to be there for my family in the way that I would like to be. I told him I am always working or with the kids. There is no time left for my grandmothers. I really resent it.

My Nano was always there for me and I hope to be there for her until the end.

At 1 PM I met my husband and his attorney at the courthouse. I do not feel happy about the financial agreement at all, but I felt like I did not have other options.

His attorney told me this is *temporary*, but somehow I feel like this is very unfair.

The most crucial thing to me was that I do not want my children spending the night with their dad until there is a proven, long-term track record of sobriety. And that was accomplished.

"Women with dependent children experience a 73 percent drop in standard of living after a divorce, while their ex-husbands' living standard goes up by 42 percent. The colloquial summing up is simpler: If women have young children, they are only one man away from welfare...Yet if two homemakers were to cross the street and work for each other's husbands, they would be entitled to an eight-hour day and a forty-hour week, Social Security, disability pay, and unemployment compensation—and perhaps paid vacations, transferable health benefits, and a retirement plan (not to mention a better legal safeguard against violence, which also has economic value). Something is very wrong here."

-Gloria Steinem, "Revaluing Economics"

I am disappointed with the initial outcome of the court hearing. I am frustrated because what I *got* and what I was *promised* were two different things. I am disappointed because I feel I have been mislead by my husband for months about his intentions. I feel defeated because I feel that I am the one who has been here doing all the work and trying to do the right thing—yet I am still the one who is getting screwed.

The judge said that we should leave this marriage on equal footing. Right now, that is not even remotely happening. My husband did not input his accurate earnings in the calculation section. The judge said we would need to have full disclosure prior to settlement, and *hopefully* that will happen.

I am fully aware that from the get-go, I have done 95% or more of all of the work relating to our children and our home.

For a long time, I considered that as my "job" or "contribution," and I was more than happy to do it.

But how is it that I am now supposed to do *even more* of the work with a very small "salary" that is now called "Alimony" and "Child

Support?" Neither of these comes close to covering our *actual* expenses.

I suppose now at least I can count on my payments and do not have to hound my (soon to be ex) husband for money to pay our bills.

I am not satisfied with this temporary agreement. I can see now why women continually stay in bad marriages.

That said, children suffer the most from all of this.

I suppose I could make the "choice" to work long hours and be the sole parent responsible for these children AND work 60+ hours a week, but *that* is not going to serve my children.

And I suppose I could "choose" to marry another man right away to take care of the three of us, but *that* is not going to serve my children.

What serves my children is having their dad buck up and take full financial responsibility for the children he fathered.

I value my job as their mother. There is nothing in the world I would rather do.

But that does not pay the bills.

It is mandatory for both parents to attend a "parenting class" to divorce in the county we live in. I'm all for being the best you can be in anything you do, but this is starting to hit a nerve.

For one, I have already read *Helping Your Kids Cope with Divorce the Sandcastles Way*, which I felt really guided me through this particular topic.

I have also been taking my son to counseling sessions nearly every week for the last two years. In that time, I have spent many hour-long one-on-one sessions with his counselor to help me to determine how to best parent both of my children through this separation and divorce—and provide guidance on how to live with my husband's addictions.

Secondly, I have the children 99% of the time. For me to go to a parenting class, I have to find someone to watch my children at the end of a long day. This means I also have to miss the most significant part of our day in terms of eating dinner together, reading books, singing songs, bathing and all the other things that make up our nightly ritual.

My husband's attorney pulled a cheap shot in court yesterday when she made a point to tell the judge that I had not been to parenting class yet.

I only was served the documents two weeks ago for the divorce he filed for seven months ago. My husband handed me *some* documents in October, but has continually told me that he wants to *try to work things out*.

My husband told me if I went to the parenting class I would know how important it is for him to spend time with the kids.

Later, my husband called me again and I really couldn't tell what he was getting at so I just said, *well, have a good night*.

He said something about me wanting to get off the phone with him so I said, "I don't know what else to say to you."

So he said, "How about I love you and I made a huge mistake?"

What mistake did I make?

He said, "Not trying to work things out with me."

So I just said, "OK, talk to you tomorrow."

He told me this was my "last chance" and that he wasn't going to ask me again.

"Contrary to what we may have been taught to think, unnecessary and unchosen suffering wounds us but need not scar us for life. It does mark us. What we allow the mark of our suffering to become is in our own hands."

-bell hooks, *All About Love*

My counselor passed away Saturday night. I had known it was coming for a while so I feel at peace with it. She was a tremendous force in my life. I began seeing her early on in my relationship with my husband. Once I realized I was pregnant with my son, I went into turbo-charge in my sessions. I really wanted to be the best possible parent I could be and I knew to do that I had things I needed to deal with first. I really credit her for helping me become the mom I am today.

When I realized I was pregnant, I knew I needed to radically change my dysfunctional default behaviors. Several co-workers were making enormous progress in their lives and they all shared one thing in common: a wise old crone named *Pat Graves*.

Pat was an unschooled, recovering alcoholic and non-traditional therapist of sorts.

Pat was prickly. She was not an easy person and I rarely looked forward to meeting her, although I loved her tremendously. She was a no-nonsense sort of woman who didn't have time or patience to be conned. She called you on your crap and she would tell you in no uncertain terms when you were wrong.

She was just the thing I needed. After years of on-and-off therapy, she would often tell me, "You've come a long way kiddo, but you still have a l-o-n-g way to go."

Pat gave me the "After A While" poem about eight years ago. It has always been special to me.

> *And you learn that you really can endure*
> *you really are strong*
> *you really do have worth*
> *and you learn*
> *with every goodbye, you learn...*
> -Veronica Shoftsall

"The end of consumerism and accumulation is the beginning of the joy of living."

-Vandana Shiva

I have been weeding out all my extras in my life these last few years. It started several years ago with the budget. I thought months ago I was down pretty good, but I decided last night there was more I could cut. I want to be comfortable, without the stress of worrying every month. No "extra" is worth that.

Every night, I read to my kids. Usually I get a few good books in, but a lot of it is "junk." It struck me last night that I am the parent and I have more control than I give myself credit. After the kids went to bed, I took all of the books out that I didn't feel represented my values. That was *most* of them. I put them under my daughter's bed for now, and if there is a major meltdown about one or two, they might magically reappear. But my kids are bombarded with messages that don't support their growth, and books should be a more positive aspect.

I have been tired and overworked as a single mom, so a lot of this has slid, especially lately. But not anymore.

I am trying to find some good shots of my wedding dress. I have been trying to sell it unsuccessfully on eBay for weeks now. I am trying to sell everything I can so we can get by until my income is steady and good enough to support all three of us.

It's funny the things that you hold onto and you think you can't do without for so long. I didn't ever think I would sell my wedding rings. I was so attached to those diamonds. But now I see that all these pretty things have cost me so much.

My daughter broke the Tiffany China plate I bought her as a baby a few weeks ago. It made me realize that even the things that we cling to and don't want to let go of can be taken away in an instant. So it is better to realize that and just let go willingly. *What are all these things if I can't take care of my children?*

I have been cleaning out my office and my computer all day. I've gone through thousands of pictures on my hard drive. It's amazing to see all the stuff I have accumulated over the last six years.

It's nostalgic and sad, but also liberating to throw so much out. I think I have a tendency to hold on to too much.

I have been feeling bogged down for a long time. I feel like I need to clean out everything from my life, whether it be diet, "stuff" or toxic people.

"Three things cannot be long hidden: the sun, the moon, and the truth."

-Buddha

This is not a happy day for me.

Last night, I was checking my Facebook account when I saw a notification pop up that two of my friends had been tagged in a picture. Usually I wouldn't probably have taken notice, but for whatever reason it intrigued me and I clicked on the link.

The picture was of my husband and one of his "friends"—both with a big glass of wine in their hands. My husband's eyes look messed up. It occurred to me that while I do drink alcohol, you would be hard-pressed to find a picture of me where my eyes look like this.

There have been so many signs of my husband's drinking—for months, if not years.

I have always been made out to be the "crazy" one. My husband always denies everything. I have smelled alcohol on his breath, he is late, the finances are a mess, he doesn't show up for things...

All the signs have been there. But to see this picture, was just a hard slap in the face. I felt like I had been knocked down to my knees.

The picture was taken last July, weeks after our camping trip with his AA group. This is significant because my husband had announced his AA sobriety birthday the January prior.

Obviously, that was not the case.

At first, I felt somewhat vindicated. The reason for our separation last May was because he did not come home all night long. A few weeks after that, he missed our daughter's third birthday entirely.

I told his family that I thought he was drinking and gave them my reasons why. That birthday party was actually the last day I saw his aunt alive. She was clearly upset. But later, his dad sided with my husband, and I suppose the rest of the family did too.

My father-in-law told me, "Maybe if you were nicer to your husband, he would come home more often."

All these years, he has enabled my husband. My father-in-law has too much vested in believing that his son is right, and I am wrong.

It really saddens me that after all of these rehabs, AA and everything else that my husband is still not sober. I have always rooted for him, even if I was not able to stand by him anymore. I have been angry, so angry—but now I am just sad.

"Pleasure is a vital nutrient."

-Christiane Northrup, M.D.

I stopped into see some of my Lebanese friends with my daughter this morning at their donut shop. I didn't know who would be there exactly but I lucked out and saw three of my favorite people. They gave us a huge box of donuts and we started talking and laughing. My favorite, Haj, who is the patriarch of the family, came in and immediately smiled. He told me that the last time I ran into him at Costco, he did not even recognize me. I had lost so much weight that I was *extremely* thin. He said he walked out the door and asked his daughter, "W*ho was that?*"

When she told him it was *me* he could not believe it.

He said, "Now you are back. I'm so happy!"

He asked about my marriage and I told him I was getting a divorce. He said he had heard that and was sorry. He said my daughter was beautiful and he wished her good luck. He said in Lebanon, when they see a beautiful young girl, they always wish her luck to marry a kind man.

He said, "Not everyone is lucky like me in business and love." He began to speak of his wife who passed many years ago after a very bad stroke. He shared a story about sending her to Lebanon once for vacation while they were living in Africa. Israel invaded the south of Lebanon a few days after she arrived. Members of the Israeli Army came into their home and demanded all the gold and valuables. They took all her paperwork. It took 3 years before she was able to return to him.

I met his family more than 15 years ago. His wife was extremely disabled from a stroke when I met her. She had to be fed, could not walk, and could barely speak. The grace that her family took care of her during that 10-year period before she died has always stayed with me. Her daughter-in-law would quietly wipe away her drool when no one was looking. She had to be helped with every little thing in her day-to-day life. But I always remember that they treated her with dignity, respect and love. I never heard anyone in that family complain, even though I knew they were very hard duties to carry out day-to-day for all those years.

Even now after her death—nearly six years ago—he was still obviously deeply in love with his wife.

Then he spoke of his daughters. He has five.

He said all but one were lucky with their husbands because they asked his blessing first. The daughter that did not get his blessing married a very bad man who did not work and lived off of her. He told her that he did not believe she should marry him, but she decided she wanted to anyway. He told me about a recent fight they had where the husband called him and threatened to divorce his daughter. He told him, "Please do!" And began to laugh.

I promised, "Next time, I will bring my man to you first to check him out." We laughed again.

Haj got up to leave and gave me a giant hug. He told me, "You are a very nice girl. You deserve a lot better. I love you."

"To be fully alive, fully human, and completely awake is to be continually thrown out of the nest."

-Pema Chodron, *When Things Fall Apart*

I have been mentally preparing the kids for the time that we will leave our home and move into something much smaller. I have come to terms with that. This is a large home to manage on my own, especially with the children, who need a lot of care and love —and also are prone to make messes the moment I clean something.

The irony is not lost on me that I have spent the last two years helping people stay in their homes, and I will lose mine.

I have spent the last 12 years helping hundreds of people improve their credit, and my credit is now tanked.

I have done all of this without cost to anyone or profit to me because it is something I believe in strongly. I used to think credit was an indication of character, and it sometimes is. However, over the years I also found that many people were hit by forces they could not control. I always tried to help those people.

Yesterday a man called to ask me to help him with his credit. I called him back and told him my grandmother was dying and I was not available. I know I am doing the right thing now, but I was also sad that I could not even refer him to someone else. I tried to explain that it was never part of my job; it was just something I did. I don't know any other brokers who do this for people.

Ironically, I also helped my husband improve his credit, which was very bad when I met him. Despite this, he seems to have no problem leaving me with this mess. He will always have his dad to bail him out and pay cash for anything. I don't have that option.

It is a hard thing to grapple with, partly because my ego is still attached to it. I took pride in my good credit. I took pride in my home. And now both will soon be gone.

But I do believe that better things will come. A credit score is only a picture in time. It is never static and I can work to improve it. And I know I will be happier living somewhere else.

It's funny how losing things has shown me some of the lies I so eagerly believed.

I was so attached to my beautiful diamonds. It was so hard to take them off my finger. But now I rarely wear rings at all. I appreciate the simplicity of my fingers. I don't want another ring there. The rings now represent a false promise. My husband was never committed to me. The rings only represented that I was *his*. I was a possession. The rings were a reflection of *him*, not of me.

My children do not want to leave this home. It is all they have really known. I am sad for them, but I am trying to paint a happy picture filled with new possibilities and dreams.

I have been looking through many of the old pictures from my childhood. Some of the most comforting photos are of me in my grandparents' home. My parents moved around after they divorced, so my grandparent's home was a rock for me. I realized it was just the familiarity that meant so much to it—because it was their home and it was filled with so much love.

The kids and I spent some time helping out at the church this morning with the grounds upkeep. I spent most of my time weeding. I got to thinking that weeding is a lot like getting rid of things you don't want in your life. I started out in the most obvious place, a huge patch of weeds surrounding a tree. There were so many there that I didn't notice all the other weeds elsewhere. Once I finished pulling those, the other weeds were more apparent. There were a lot—everywhere! And, next week, there will be more again.

It's easy to get frustrated about this, but that's just life.

For a long time my husband and I had gardeners—most of our neighbors did as well. I was thinking today how peaceful I felt working in the dirt. It's a shame many of us have gotten away from doing that. I think it's a good way to reconnect with yourself —and the earth.

There were at least 30 other people there helping. I was also thinking how nice it was to have so many people pitching in. It reminded me that people will help you—if you ask.

"Psychic numbing means never having to feel anything. Refusing such anesthetization and unearthing our passions means facing our emotions, especially those that have been the most anathematized, such as rage, female pride, and self-love. In short, it entails embracing monsters... Yet those of us who are sick of pretending, denying, suppressing, and repressing our knowledge, our emotions, and our powers journey to her island of rock and stone and there face a laughing, welcoming, and gorgeous Gorgon. As we do, we turn not to stone, but to sentient flesh, sensual mind, and boiling blood."

-Jane Caputi, *Gossips, Gorgons and Crones*

I firmly believe that the only way out of all of this is leaving the dysfunctional relationship behind—as much as possible. In my case, there are children, so my ex will always be somehow involved in my life.

But to live day-to-day, as I had been living—even separated—is not conceivable to me any longer.

I don't want to end up like my grandmother, dying too young from cancer, after 36 years married to an alcoholic. She sacrificed herself to him and to her family. It was the only choice for her in her day, and I ache for her. I ache for all women who have been in relationships with addicts. It is hell. *Pure hell*.

I don't believe that traditional recovery groups are the answer. I believe 12-step groups are deeply flawed, especially for women.

The thing I saw meeting after meeting for 95% of people is not what I would call "recovery." It was recycling the same garbage. Putting up with very poor behavior and then venting about it. *Yes*, it is an outlet, and *yes*, it is better than nothing. But after all this time, we need to do better. We need better programs that are progressive and deal with the specific needs of women.

The advice I would give to any woman who asked me what to do if she were in my shoes is to leave the relationship and work on herself. An alcoholic, "recovering" or not, will drain you. My definition of recovery has completely changed as well over the years, and it does not have much to do with never-ending 12-step meetings.

Recovery for me has meant joy—pure joy. Not repeating meeting lingo or being how someone thinks I should be. I feel that I have *finally* come home to myself. I believe that I am good and deserve to be happy.

For so long I was scared to leave. But it was the best thing I ever did—for my children and me as far as I am concerned. I am happier than I have been for a long time. I actually have energy to focus on things that I enjoy. I have renewed energy to volunteer, which has also been enormously healing for me. How wonderful to focus on someone who *wants* your help—that will truly benefit. An alcoholic can only help himself when *he* is ready.

I am sad for all the tears I shed and wasted energy I spent over the years. *But I have learned.*

> "Inherited wealth and power enforce patriarchy pure,
> and envy of this ladylike trap makes the rest of us
> behave against our own best interests."
>
> -Gloria Steinem

I went to a ladies lunch on Thursday at the home of a good friend of mine. I was planning to just pop by, as I don't usually do a three-hour lunch. But the time flew by and I found myself enjoying it.

I have not been around people with money for a while. Perhaps I have been avoiding it in my own way. But I do love my friend.

It's funny—when I met her, I assumed a lot about her because of the way she dressed, mostly. She is completely entrenched in upscale brand names. I remember I started doing that for a while and my sister commented that I was becoming a walking advertisement.

After a year of getting to know my friend, I found there is a lot that lies beneath the surface. She is a very sweet and thoughtful person. She has had struggles of her own that no one would ever suspect.

I think women with money have the same or more hindrances as most women. But they are expected to be a certain way—*act like a lady—dress well—keep their shape—take care of all the social obligations, to help promote her husband's career*. And the majority of them live up to this image, especially when they marry into money. All of these expectations take up a lot of time. They also detract from the full creative potential and individual economic well-being of the woman.

Money protects its own. If the woman does not live up to this image created for her, there will not be a place for her—and she will not have the skills needed to go out on her own. And in most cases, she will not be able to enjoy the same lifestyle if the relationship ends. Hence, she is in her own cage—a very pretty bird with no place to go.

For years I wore a size zero and most of the women surrounding me wore a similar size. It seemed normal and expected.

I am now at a size 4 and I was easily the biggest woman there. It was a strange position to be in after being away from it. No one said anything directly, but one woman did say she didn't recognize me when she first walked in.

I am glad to have my curves back. I don't want to be a size 0 anymore. For a woman who is 5'7", coming from a voluptuous family, that size is just plain crazy.

Being that thin was never intentional for me. I think primarily it was the result of stress and extended breastfeeding. I felt the worst I have ever felt in my life—but in those circles, everyone constantly told me how amazing I looked. My family and friends kept me sane.

The biggest question the women had for me was how it felt to be without my rings. It was the first time people have been so candid with me about this. It was a very interesting conversation and probably not one I would have in most places. All of them had large diamonds as well. They wanted to know how I felt without mine. They could not *imagine* taking theirs off.

I thought that was a very valid and interesting perspective. A large ring almost always enslaves you to a man. And, it becomes part of who you are—as they all affirmed. In many ways, a large ring speaks for you in ways words cannot.

I explained that it was difficult for me and it was a *process*. This was the first time I have felt that everyone in the room knew exactly what I was talking about.

It is one thing to say that you would just throw a large diamond off your finger. It is *quite* another one to wear one for a long time and choose to take it off. I *loved* my rings. They were beautiful.

But, I explained that I now prefer my fingers without any rings on them. And that I realized my ring represented a false promise, and a false life.

People see a ring like that and they make a lot of assumptions about who you are. And even if you do have a "good" marriage, I think many of those assumptions are wrong. At least they were for me.

Everywhere you go, the first thing people see is the size of your ring. It detracts from who *you* are as a person. I finally feel like I am *me*.

The second thing that came out of that lunch is something that has been evolving in me for a long time.

As women, we grow up hearing a lot of advertisements about makeup, skin care and "beauty." The assumption is that if we spend all this time and money to look a certain way, our lives will be wonderful. All of this amounts to so much wasted time and resources, and our lives are no better for it.

I don't want to play the game anymore.

Most of these products are pumped with chemicals and toxins. In fact, if you wear heavy makeup, especially starting at a young age, it will actually make you look older.

The incidence of skin cancer is through the roof. And I believe a lot of this is not necessarily from the sun, but the products we use on our skin —including most sunscreen.

There are products without all this crap in them, and I am learning more about them. I mix my own oils, made with completely natural organic oils. This is a very inexpensive way to moisturize your skin. And it works beautifully.

I don't want to even spend the time dying my hair anymore. What is wrong with gray hair? *Nothing!* Is it worth seeping toxins into my skull?

I have a friend who is just a few years older than me and she does not dye her hair. She assumed she was older than me when we met, but I did not think that. I thought her hair looked lovely and she inspired me to stop dying mine.

My mother has a glorious gray mane. For years she spent tons of time and money trying to get it dyed a certain color. It never held the color right and detracted from her beauty. I think she looks lovelier than ever now.

I think one of the biggest reasons that women spend so much time and money on these products is that we somehow feel we are in competition with each other. *We are not.* We need to spend more time supporting and loving each other. When more of us stop playing this ridiculous game, more women will find the courage to live as they are. Men do not spend the same time and energy on their appearance. No one thinks they need to. *What makes females innately wrong as we are?*

I have never worn a lot of makeup, but lately I wear less and less. As I told my friends the other day: *everything* is on the table now. I am reconsidering all of it. I want to spend my life in creative endeavors, doing things that support my children and me. Anything that does not support that dream is *off* the table.

"The most potent weapon in the hands of the oppressor is the mind of the oppressed."

-Steve Biko

Tonight I am reeling after a day full if reeling.

I received paperwork from my husband's attorney late last week. There was a small line in the documents that said if I did not respond within 30 days of being served, he would automatically win the case.

This was after picking up my daughter for him, as he was *unable* to do it.

I asked my husband about this and he said I had *nothing to worry about*. He said he called his attorney and she affirmed that I had already appeared in the case and did not need to do anything further.

Since my husband has proven to be a habitual liar, I decided to go to the courthouse myself with my own document to respond.

I waited and waited in a second line after the security check line. It was hot and I ended up taking my coat off. I felt like I was going to have a heart attack. My heart was beating faster and faster and the line seemed to never move.

After about 45-minutes of waiting, I finally got to a clerk and asked if my document would work. *Her face fell*. She told me *no*. She looked up my information and saw when I was served and when I was expected to respond and her jaw kept dropping. She said that I did, in fact, need to appear or the case would be decided as *my husband's attorney had written it*, which includes joint custody of our children. It also includes his delusional attempt of portraying his income, which will determine child support and alimony. I started crying as I told her my husband is an addict and I could not let that happen.

She gave me the proper forms to file and a waiver form for the $300+ filing fee.

Thank God for intuition. I still have to say *it hurts*. After all I have suffered with my husband I was still gullible enough to believe him. I was still foolish enough to believe he wanted the best for the kids and me. I was still stupid enough to believe he wanted to work this out amicably.

It will be a long time before I believe another word that comes out of his mouth.

I spent most of the night gathering my documents and filling in the necessary forms. My dad watches my son on Tuesdays so he went over all the documents with me to make sure I did not miss anything.

I barely slept. I kept thinking of new things I needed to include. I also had a presentation with my son at his school early the next morning. I knew I would have to drop my daughter off at early care, get to my son's school and try to make the presentation fun, and then finish what I needed to do for court by 11 AM.

The presentation at my son's school went well and I tried to stay calm as I prepared all the documents at my office and made all the necessary copies. At the last minute, I found a notary who was happy to help me. (I was literally walking out the door, late.)

I went down to the courthouse at the time I was supposed to be there and was told that they didn't have time to help me because they were going to close for lunch in 20 minutes. She told me to come back in about an hour. I decided to try to eat something, but I could not.

I went back and stood in line. I was the first one so I was able to see the clerk first. I thought I had all my documentation ready but he seemed perplexed by something. It seems that he thought my expenses were inconsistent with my income and that raised a red flag for fraud.

At that point, I lost it. I could not hold the tears back. He asked me if I had documentation of my mortgage, and I did not think I did. I was just about to give up when I remembered that I had pulled a copy of my credit report that morning to show the damage that has been done to my credit history.

Then, I started bawling right there in the courthouse lobby. It was one of the most humiliating moments of my life.

The clerk was able to use my information and grant me the waiver. He obviously felt bad for me—and gave me some tissues and tried to make me laugh.

I went into the next line to wait. That was somewhat less humiliating, although I was still in the same lobby with all the same people who had just witnessed me sobbing.

The clerk had me help him paper-punch all the documents, told me I was *done* and wished me *good luck*.

I think I did everything correctly. It will be interesting what the response from my husband and his attorney will be. Neither knows I filed yet. I suppose they think they will have an automatic win tomorrow. Instead, they will get copies of my response.

"The best thing you could do is master the chaos in you.
You are not thrown into the fire, you are the fire."

-Mama Indigo

We had our first joint mediation session today. It was emotionally draining for me.

I realize I will have to compromise on many things but there is a lot that is still very hard for me to swallow.

My husband has not been taking the kids during the times that he *said* he *wanted*. Today, he asked for more time, including overnights.

We left the session angry. We both were upset throughout the session, although I think the mediator did a good job of keeping us both grounded. At one point, my husband nearly walked out, but the mediator got him to sit back down and finish the session.

I know this will be tough to get through. All the particulars are emotional—money, debt that neither of us can pay ourselves, who gets what holidays with the children, the safety of the kids with their dad...

After going through this I would say that in *almost* every case, a divorce is not the way to go. Certainly *no one* wins. But in my case, I wish I had done it sooner. I feel like the longer I stayed, the more screwed I got.

"It is easier to build strong children than to repair broken men."
-Frederick Douglass

My husband was supposed to pick our son up from school yesterday. He called me after mediation, after reiterating his commitment to keeping his commitments to the kids, and said he would like to switch days.

So, I went to pick up my son. His face fell as soon as he saw me.

Once in the car, he started crying.

When I tried to talk to him about it he started yelling at me.

I asked him what I could do to make him feel better. He shouted, "Nothing."

He said he had been looking forward to seeing his dad all day.

He cried for 15 minutes. It broke my heart. I asked him if he wanted a hug. He yelled NO. Everything I tried to help him fell flat.

I decided to pick my daughter up late and spend a little extra time with my son. She has aftercare available and was not expecting her dad. We went and got ice cream. He ordered his first double scoop.

My husband got mad at me when I told him. He said, "*My* heart is broken... It would mean a lot to me if you could support me and help to explain that nothing is more important to me than them, but sometimes Daddy has to work for our family."

"Once upon a time, when women were birds, there was the simple understanding that to sing at dawn and to sing at dusk was to heal the world through joy. The birds still remember what we have forgotten, that the world is meant to be celebrated."

-Terry Tempest Williams

I didn't sleep well last night but my days keep getting better and better. I decided to take a walk in the gorgeous spring sunshine and clear my head. While I was out, my first husband's father-in-law called me and asked what I was doing.

He wanted to have me over for dinner. I already had plans with my sister and my office, but it was so thoughtful of him to call. It made my day. I kept telling him I had plans and he would say, "Come anyway! Bring your sister! Bring your office! Just come! We're making kebabs!"

Everything I have learned about happiness, I learned from the Lebanese. I think it was in my nature as a child to be sad. But there was always a part of me that loved to be silly and laugh. After being around the Lebanese—and spending time in Lebanon especially—I saw that many people have every reason to sit around and be sad. *But they don't.* They laugh, they tease, they eat, they sing—they enjoy their lives.

My first husband taught me to push out whatever was not helping me and pull in that which was. Whenever I come to him with a problem, he almost always says, "*Who cares!*" He always gets me to see that in the scheme of things, my life is bigger than my small problem at that moment. And then, he laughs—and *usually*, I do too.

Losing My Grandmothers & Finding My Mother

"The voice of women and the voice of nature have been muted under patriarchy. Women and nature are considered objects under patriarchy, and objects do not speak, objects do not feel, and objects have no needs. Objects exist only to serve the needs of others."

-Marti Kheel

When I was a child, there was nothing I liked more than to cook with my dad's mom. I still have many of her hand-written recipes after all these years; although most of them I know by heart.

My paternal grandparents were married happily for nearly 65 years. My Pappa died in 2007. He had just turned 90 and continued to work until the last 2 months of his life. My family all was there with him that entire time so he could die at home as he wished. I will always be grateful for those last months with him— and for the tremendous man he was in my life.

After so many years together, most people assumed my Nano, who had always been the more fragile in health, would soon pass. She gave us another three years.

One of my fondest memories of Nano was at a dinner a few weeks after my grandpa died. It had been a rough patch for her and my aunt Norma had come out to help. I thought she would just give up and die. For whatever, reason, she perked up at this dinner and I saw this completely quirky and joyous side of her that had never come out before. This continued to come out in various ways for years. It was a gift I will always cherish.

"Within the war we are all waging with the forces of death, subtle and otherwise, conscious or not – I am not only a casualty, I am also a warrior."

-Audre Lorde

My grandmother has been in the hospital since Monday night. I have been with her most of the daytime hours.

My heart has been heavy.

I left at 5 PM today, as one of my sisters was able to come down from Seattle to be with my grandmother. My dad and I had been with her most of the time until then. I did not want to leave her alone. She is almost 93.

I have been on the fence about what to do about my job for a while. I have known I did not want my current position and met with my supervisor last week. He was very generous with me and I have been weighing what he said since then.

However, this morning, during my grandmother's procedure, I realized my heart is just not there, and I did not want to stay.

I resigned today.

I have been at my job for nearly six years, so it was a hard decision.

Both of my grandmothers and my great-grandmother are now terminal.

My financial position is not great right now—I suppose that is all relative—but I just feel that I need this time with these women who have been so fundamental to me in my own life.

Caregiving is not a respected "job" in our society. Much like motherhood, it is not valued, because it is not a paid position. But to me, there is no more important job in the world.

I have had some very intimate moments with my grandmother these last few days—time that money could never buy or even approach.

I have been very strong all week. I have tried to be lighthearted and laugh with my grandmother. Tonight, I took a break and took my children to an Earth Day concert with African music. Perhaps that broke me. My children have missed me. My mother and their father have done a good job helping me this week. But the children are used to me. They were needy and did not behave their best. My daughter loved the music, but my son pouted. I did not have my usual patience.

I broke down and cried on the way home. It has been a long week. And I know there is more to come. Both my sisters live in Seattle, so the burden is mostly on my dad and me. I am glad to take it, but it is also exhausting.

I try to express to my children the importance of what I am doing, but I don't think they understand. I realized tonight at the hippie gathering that we attended that my children do not share all of my values. Perhaps I have done a poor job of expressing them, or perhaps there have been too many outside influences. But I really want them to understand that money is not the savior of the world. *Love is*. Family *is*.

In the end, that is all there is. And if you don't know that, you will be lost.

"Pain and pleasure go together; they are inseparable. They can be celebrated. They are ordinary. Birth is painful and delightful. Death is painful and delightful. Everything that ends is also the beginning of something else. Pain is not a punishment; pleasure is not a reward."

-Pema Chodron, *When Things Fall Apart*

Another day at the hospital with my grandmother and her impending death is bringing up so many things for me.

My husband has tried to be supportive of me and I appreciate that. But I cannot help but remember how he responded while my grandpa was dying.

I thought I had gotten over that, but I have not. I still am resentful. I think, *why is he suddenly being so nice now when we are nearly divorced*?

When I suffered a miscarriage—in the midst of caring for my dying grandfather—he was not supportive at all. As I sobbed, he sneered, "Get off the cross—someone needs the wood."

Yesterday a woman that I adore from church, who is much older than me and has known my grandparents for 30 years, told a story that brought back that memory.

She talked about how after her second divorce, she decided to rename herself. And she took away her middle and last names, and gave herself the middle name of the daughter she had miscarried and a new last name.

It was a beautiful name.

That resonated so well with me. I still think about that child a lot, and to me, she was a girl, and she would have been named *Grace*.

My grandmother and I spoke today about the wars in Iraq and Afghanistan—and their utter meaninglessness to both of us. Those of us in the United States cling to our own lives so dearly. We will do anything to avoid dying. And yet we seem to have no problem with the deaths of "others" who we perceive to be so different from us.

When I was in Lebanon, one of the hardest things for me to deal with was learning about the death of my first husband's childhood best friend. He was only eight-years-old when the Israeli soldiers killed him.

I will never forget going to his parent's home. *The way his father sobbed*. And then I sobbed—and Hussein sobbed.

But I could not stop.

I remember that my sister-in-law came to me in my room after hours of this. She took me square by the shoulders, looked me in the eyes, and said, "Everyone dies. *Everyone* dies."

I have never forgotten those words. I have never forgotten how *senseless* his death felt. And I think if more Americans saw that, they would realize that war is *never* a good idea.

My sister-in-law's words have carried me through a lot of deaths though over the years. We have a culture here in the US that does not acknowledge or accept death. But death is inevitable for all of us.

The combination of the fear of death and medicine for profit is a very bad mix.

I spoke to my other grandma at length last night. She told me again that she plans to just be here and happy with all of us one week and be "gone" the next. She refused chemotherapy or any other treatment. She just wants to be as healthy as possible, naturally, for as long as she can. And then, she will *chose* her time.

My paternal grandma thought that was horrible, but I relate to that more. I don't want to live on 15 medications on a good day. *That is not life.* My grandma is nearly 93-years-old. Some of the things they are suggesting for her are insane. That's not even humane in my mind. But she is afraid. And fear makes for good profits.

None of us has greater or lesser worth. The death of one person is just as painful for their loved-ones as my grandmothers' deaths will be for me.

I can accept the deaths of the matriarchs of my family. But I know how hard for me it has been to lose a child that essentially never even *existed*. I have never been able to make peace with wars that kill children.

"The mysteries are what is wild in us, what cannot be quantified or contained. But the mysteries are also what is common to us all: blood, breath, heartbeat, the sprouting of seed, the waxing and waning of the moon, the turning of the earth around the sun, birth, growth, death, renewal."

-Starhawk

My grandma died yesterday. It was very quick and peaceful. I was able to be there with her, which is what I had hoped for.

She lived a wonderful life and died a wonderful death with her family around her.

Our new pastor and many people from the church have also come by, called and emailed, and we are very grateful for that.

The theme that has continually come up during my time with her is her grace and compassion toward everyone. I saw her be so sweet and kind with every person she came in contact with. Everyone in the hospital loved her. I know she felt so awful and yet she was never in a bad mood or foul with anyone.

I told our church secretary that the story of my grandma's life was caring about everyone else. Even in her final days, she was constantly asking about other people. And I was told when one of our church members came to pray with her, she asked her to pray for *me* because she was worried about me and the kids.

We have enjoyed the time singing hymns, reading from the Bible, reading poetry and listening to my dad's music—and of course, talking about everything. It is time that can never be replaced and I am so glad that we had it.

In one of our talks she told me that she felt like she had a big role in raising us. And I agreed with that. She said, "*You had a rough run with things.*" I told her I didn't think I could have made it without her.

Nano always had very strong feelings of right and wrong. However, I have to say that I made some choices in my life that must have grated against every grain in her being. She never tried to control or sway me. She always respected and loved me through every phase of my life. And she never rubbed anything in my face.

I often think that you don't fully appreciate your family until you have your own children. I have often guessed at the sacrifices she made for me, and I'm sure I will never begin to know the extent of everything she did. A true sacrifice is never advertised; it is just what you do for your family.

I told my dad that I want nothing from my grandmother. When someone has given you so much of themselves, nothing monetary is necessary. I have my memories. I have my pictures. I have every letter and card she ever gave me since I was about seven-years-old. I have her love. I have her spirit.

I took her remaining jewelry that the family did not want to church on Sunday and let the women pick out one or two items they liked. It will be fun to see the remnants of my grandma on all the other women in the church who meant so much to her.

"Capitalism does not do life. And that lie is never more exposed in the twenty-first century than when we bring to it the light of gender and the unsaid – the silences and secrets that are knotted in the articulation of capitalism and patriarchy."

-Beatrix Campbell

Most of my experiences with my grandmother dying were positive. People seem to look at me strangely when I say that, but it is true. I knew in my heart she would die. And I knew I wanted to be there. And so, while I had a few moments of breakdowns and despair, the majority of my experience was purely positive. It was pure joy to be able to care for my grandmother in her last days. It was a gift and a blessing.

She stayed most of the last two weeks in the hospital, and that was wonderful. She received good care and was well-liked. She never complained and was always kind with everyone, so I am sure that had an effect on the care she received.

We were hoping she would not have to move. She lasted longer than we thought she would—she was stronger than any of us ever imagined in her frail, 108-pound body.

After talking to many people, it became apparent to me that, for whatever reasons, hospitals do not like people to die there. So, while I know the social workers and administrators tried to stretch her stay out as long as possible, ultimately, she had to be moved to a "rehabilitation center."

I did not want this for my grandmother, but I knew she needed more extensive nursing care than we could give her at home with hospice.

The moment I walked in there, I hated the place.

It was a "nice" place as far as that goes. One thing my family does not scrimp on, is care for our family when they need it. We are not wealthy by any means, but we take care of our family as well as possible.

It instantly struck me walking down the hall (my grandmother's room was at the very end) that this was a place people were sent to die. And most of them were completely alone. It was a depressing place. I would not want to die there.

In her room, we created our own world. We shut the door, listened to music and talked while she was able.

The first day she arrived, I had visited her in the morning before church with the children. She had moved afterwards and my sister was there with my dad and his wife, so I did not go out again. I knew she was well taken care of.

I came Monday morning as soon as I dropped both children off school. My father had been there late, so he slept in a little.

When I got there, my grandmother was severely distressed. It was a state I have rarely seen her in, except right before and after my grandfather's death.

I had to quickly compose myself so I did not lose it too.

She had been sitting there since about 4 AM without her hearing aides, so she could basically hear nothing, on top of being completely disoriented by her new surroundings. We had managed to keep track of her hearing aids for nearly two weeks in the hospital without incident.

I asked several nurses multiple times, and no one knew where they were. I searched her room three times to no avail, then texted my dad and sister to see if they knew anything. Neither of them did.

I tried to stay calm while my grandma became more and more upset. I asked her if we could purchase her a new set. She nearly started to cry and said they had to be ordered and they cost over $2,500.

My dad called the center and they managed to find them. Apparently it was their policy to hold onto them overnight, but no one told us that for more than an hour.

While we were still trying to figure that out, I tried to calm my grandma by asking what else she needed. She was always a very clean woman and felt dirty.

I told her I would bathe her and started to do so. I had done it a few times in the hospital already but she had never become comfortable with it. She is very modest. I had not seen her naked before this time. I kept joking with her and telling her it was *nothing I had not seen*. She would smile. She was always so gracious. She just kept saying, "I'm sorry. I didn't want for you to have to do this."

It became apparent that they had left her in an old soiled diaper for some time. She was so humiliated about this I nearly cried. I could not let her sit there like that. I told her I would change it. She tried to stop me but I told her I didn't mind—she had changed plenty of mine. It makes me sad that she was left with so much humiliation on her last day of awareness.

The nurse tried to say later that she had checked it earlier, but I have at least five years of diaper duty under my belt. *I know an old diaper*. What I did not know was how to change one on someone nearly as big as me who cannot move much anymore on their own. It was a struggle, but we did it. She had to help me by moving around in all sorts of ways. At least she was clean.

While I was bathing her, the maintenance man knocked at her door. She had been sitting there for 4-5 hours alone after she woke up. She had asked them to turn on her CD. No one seemed to be able to figure that out. So she asked for the TV, to have some distraction. They told her they would have to find a remote.

So here I was bathing my very modest grandmother, and this man knocks at the door while she is exposed. She had already specified she did not even want a male nurse. I tell him, "I am *bathing* her." He walks in anyway and plays around with the remote.

I don't want to upset my grandmother so I texted my dad. Luckily she did not have her hearing aides yet anyway, but I did not want the negative energy.

So the director of the place knocks and comes in. She started giving me all these excuses, as apparently my dad called her to complain. She then asks my grandmother very condescendingly if *she knows when she moves her bowels.*

At that point, I lost it. I told her to *GET OUT*. She seemed stunned and just stood there looking at me. I turned my back to her and told her three more times. *Please leave—please just leave.*

My grandma asked what she had said, but I did not have the heart to tell her.

After that, she quickly went downhill. She pretty much fell asleep except for a few brief moments. One of my sisters wanted to talk to her on the phone from Seattle. As soon as she heard her voice, she perked up and began to speak, with a huge smile on her face.

She died the next day while I was in the middle of giving her a sponge bath. The rest of the family had left to meet with the director again. I decided to stay; I was disgusted with them anyway. I came back with a final tub of clean water and started to wash her again. I noticed her breathing had slowed, and then it stopped.

What is tragic to me about all of this is that my grandmother had family with her the majority of the time before she died. She was only alone during sleeping hours and then she had nursing care.

But I rarely saw anyone visit the other patients in the hospital or the rehab center. *Everyone was alone.* And that seemed so inhumane and wrong to me.

I know that if I had not been there when I was, my grandmother's care would have been poor—as it was before I got there. It was only after my dad and I became outraged that everyone put on their best behavior.

But what about everyone else?

The best care should be the standard of care. *And where were all the families of the dying?*

"Appeals to the abuser's compassion are fruitless, because the abuser is not empathetic."

-Patricia Evans

My grandfather's funeral was ruined because of my husband and his father. My husband showed up after the service was over and his dad insisted on making a scene at the reception.

I did not want him to come to my grandmother's service because of this and he did not.

Everything went very well until after the reception. My daughter had been sick so I had kept her home from school. By 3 PM, she was *spent*. I carried her out to the car, but she had a meltdown. I do not usually wear high heels and there was a ridge in the sidewalk I tripped over. We both fell.

I tried to break her fall with my hands, so I got pretty banged up. But she still hit her head anyway, which was upsetting for both of us. I sat there for at least five minutes in a daze. No one was around us or heard us and I just didn't want to get up.

She fell asleep almost as soon as I put her in the car and I called the doctor's office. The nurse told me what to watch for. When we got home, I called her dad and gave him the instructions, as he was to pick her up after our family dinner and I did not want to forget anything. He told me that perhaps I should just *deal with it.* That was fine with me. I told him he should come pick up our son though because he gets upset when he does not.

I had made a delicious pot roast dinner. It had slow-cooked for nearly 10 hours and was probably the best one I have ever made. I had invited my close family over for a dinner after the reception. I thought it would be nice to have some private time together, and dinners were always very important to my grandma.

I set the table in the morning with the china and silver she had given me years before. I made sure everything on the table had been hers, and it made the dinner very special for all of us.

Afterward, I asked my sister's boyfriend to play the piano for us. My dad and sisters and I sang along when we knew the words. I was thinking in my head that *this was heaven*. I really felt happy and at peace.

Then my husband came.

He decided he wanted to take my daughter and she did not want to go with him. Ultimately, there was a standoff between us and he threatened to call the police.

My sister stepped in and said, "Don't you realize our grandma just died?"

My son ran inside with me. Ultimately neither of them went with him. My dad's wife started sobbing. She had never directly witnessed this side of him. I was crying, the kids were confused, my sisters were trying to comfort everyone—and my dad and my sister's boyfriend went outside and talked my husband out of calling the police or taking the kids by force.

But he came back in the morning and took both the kids. My daughter was sobbing and clinging to me. She kept saying, "I want to stay with mommy." She called me crying, which was more torture for both of us. *She wanted to come home.*

I can't figure out why he just wouldn't *let* her.

"But I, being poor, have only my dreams.
I have spread my dreams under your feet;
tread softly, because you tread on my dreams."

-Yeats

During mediation, it became painfully obvious that the only logical way to deal with our enormous debts was to file for bankruptcy. My husband and his family were not going to pay the debts and he could not file for bankruptcy himself because he already had done so recently. I did not have access to anywhere near that amount of money—or representation that could force the issue.

We agreed that my husband would pay for a bankruptcy attorney for me, but it was not a happy "choice" or even a fair compromise. I literally was left with nothing, except my car—which I sold off later—and my retirement accounts, which I was also forced to liquidate to feed my children.

When I blew up at my husband over the bankruptcy, he told me that if I had stayed married to him, he would have paid off all the debts.

I told him, "If that is the right thing to do, you should do it regardless."

After years of wearing me down, I finally met with the trustee downtown at the courthouse. I thought it would be easier than it was. I should have known it would not be easy at all.

I had been fighting this day for 2-3 years. It was never something I thought I would *ever* do in my life. But in the end, there seemed no other way.

I broke down sobbing mid-way through what I will call "The

Interrogation." The trustee did not understand how we could have burnt through so much money so fast. I gulped into a hard sob and explained that my ex-husband is an addict.

My attorney handed me tissues, but the whole pack was not enough.

Afterwards, he sat outside with me while I cried and cried. I could not stop for hours.

I gave my blood, my body and my milk for my children.

I gave my tears, my health, my youth, my pride, my time, my energy and my last penny to their father.

This was what was returned to me.

Afterwards, three of my long-time friends came and spent the weekend with me. I was embarrassed to share about my financial situation, especially with one friend who is fairly wealthy. When I told her, she paused for a second and said, "You just call us when it's time to move out of your house, and we will all be there and help you move with trucks and everything else."

"To lose a brother is to lose someone with whom you can share the experience of growing old, who is supposed to bring you a sister-in-law and nieces and nephews, creatures who people the tree of your life and give it new branches. To lose your father is to lose the one whose guidance and help you seek, who supports you like a tree trunk supports its branches. To lose your mother, well, that is like losing the sun above you. It is like losing—I'm sorry, I would rather not go on."

-Yann Martel, *Life of Pi*

Now, my maternal grandmother is dying of cancer. And it sounds as if it is getting worse sooner than we had thought.

It was interesting to me that my mom told me that my grandmother was afraid to leave my uncle behind.

My uncle injured his back in his twenties and should have been in a wheel chair long ago according to most of his doctors. He is in constant pain, which is unfortunate. But he drinks too much and takes it out on my grandma, who he lives with. My grandma is one of the strongest women I have ever known. But I have seen her reduced to quiet tears by my uncle on a few occasions.

I adore my uncle. He's my favorite, too. But it makes me cry just to think about this.

My family is not prone to cruelty. This grandma (Nana) curses like a sailor but she has never been unkind to me or anyone that I can think of. She is direct—always direct—but never unkind. My uncle has never been cruel to my children or me. He is always kind to us no matter how intense his pain is.

I know he loves my grandma more than anything or anyone. He adores and worships her. And yet, somehow—I suppose like most people—when he is angry, his most beloved gets the brunt of it.

I have this theory about women living with alcoholics and the pain it causes them. I know so many who ended up with cancer, like my grandma. They *take it* and *take it*. It makes me very sad.

My grandma was not one for religion or Al-Anon. She said she could barely stand all the people in Al-Anon sitting around complaining about their problems. She has no patience for that. She just always got up and did the work that raising five children took. Perhaps she shut off her emotions, but I admire her in so many ways.

She also always took care of herself very well. Most days she walked and swam—but she also took up all sorts of exercise from Tai Chi to dancing. She ate well and drank moderately. She did smoke, but disciplined herself to just a few cigarettes a day.

My paternal grandmother (Nano) was not nearly as healthy—although she and Pappa were both avid gardeners, and I think the fresh foods and exercise was great for both of them. But they lived into their 90's, whereas my mom's mother is only 72. *Too young to die.*

I was thinking the other day that my dad's mom had so much love from my grandpa—so much support. No one thought she would live this long, as she has had a heart condition for nearly 45 years. But love does wonders, whereas abuse kills.

And the difference it comes down to for me is that my dad's mother was able to live her life fully, in love and acceptance. Whereas my maternal grandma had to struggle every day to carve out a life for herself in spite of her circumstances.

Both managed to have good lives, but it was so much harder for my mom's mother.

I have been trying to make a point to spend more time with her. I stopped by the other day for lunch and headed back out again with my children on Saturday. I feel very fortunate for the love of both my grandmothers. Being a child of divorce myself, I know it was their support that held my life together at times.

I have often thought about my son and my relationship in terms of my grandmother and my uncle.

It is hard to be a single mother. And I think that women married to alcoholics are usually single mothers, whether they are divorced or not.

You rely more on your children, which is in some ways unfair to them. I struggle between making sure my children are responsible and contribute to the family—and making sure that they also get to be children and have fun.

With my grandma and my uncle, I see them both rely on each other so much. In some ways, it is so beautiful. In other ways, I am sure it has been hard on both of them.

I used to be so afraid of death and of losing someone that I love. Over the last four years or so, I have lost 16 friends and family members. It sort of all happened at once and it was hard. But what came out of it was acceptance about death.

> "My anger has meant pain to me but it has also meant survival, and before I give it up I'm going to be sure that there is something at least as powerful to replace it on the road to clarity."
>
> -Audre Lorde

I woke today feeling very frustrated. The divorce has changed *nothing*. My ex is still treating me like his wife. He is still trying to get back together in his own backwards way. I suppose he thinks I am his to have because of the child support and alimony he is paying.

I reminded him yesterday that if I weren't here taking care of the kids 24-7, he would have to hire three nannies to pay for multiple "shifts" and would pay more than triple the amount he is paying to me.

How can you shortchange the mother of your children?

He walks around with wads of $100 bills but fails to pay the bills that come for him to our home—bills that are still in both of our names. I don't have the extra money to pay for his expenses.

When something breaks, he tells me to have one of my boyfriends pay to get it fixed. Who is responsible for our house: him or my supposed boyfriends?

I am very sick of being chastised by my ex-husband for things that are *none* of his business.

I have not violated my sense of morality or ethics. I am not going to play a stupid game with him that he never seems to tire of. He continues to read my blog and picks out any segment on my sexuality to nit-pick at me. It is so childish.

He tells me almost every day that he is "done" with me or that he's "had it."

I reminded him yesterday that we filed for divorce more than a year ago and it was finalized a while ago—so the time for being "done" was over.

I need and deserve to have my peace.

I am glad to be nearly done with this. It has been a long road. It has now been over three years since my husband's relapse; two-and-a-half since our initial separation—and more than a year since the divorce was filed. That's a long time to live in limbo.

"Women's most feared power over men is the power to say no. To refuse to take care of men. To refuse to service them sexually. To refuse to buy their products. To refuse to worship their God. To refuse to love them. Every therapist knows that sex can be forced, but no power in the world can force love from any woman who wishes to withhold it."

-Barbara Walker, *The Crone*

I went to Seattle last night for my sister's 25th birthday. As I was getting out of the car when I got home, I saw my husband pulling up behind me. He must have been either circling the house or waiting up the street where I could not see him. He started screaming and yelling at me.

First he asked how my time was and I said it was good. He asked who I went with and I said *my sisters*. He said, "Who else?" I told him it was *none of his business.* He kept screaming and calling me a *fucking slut* and a *liar*. I was embarrassed so I unlocked the door and went into the house.

He followed me in and became more and more irate. He was shaking violently. He kept saying, "W*as it good, was it good? Just tell me and I will leave you alone forever*."

I told him I wasn't *going to tell him anything*.

He sneered, "I hope he had a big cock. Did he have a big cock?" He grabbed my crotch and started yelling, "Did he put it in there?" He backed me into the wall, still shaking and scary. He grabbed my butt and pulled me and jeered, "Did he grab your ass like that?"

I told him *he needed to calm down*. He asked me, "Aren't you ashamed of yourself?"

128

He must have called me a *slut* 100 times. I told him, "You are not in any position to judge anything I do. We are finished."

I told him I was going to *call the police* but I couldn't get to my phone while he was cornering me.

Then I told him that all the neighbors had heard him and he needed to go because he already had a felony conviction and if the police were called he would be in trouble.

He finally left.

After everything that he has put me through these last seven years, he thinks he is entitled to harass me. He thinks I should feel bad. He thinks that it's my fault. *Everything is always my fault.*

And I just wonder when he will grow up and move on.

Instead he called and texted me all day long.

Among the 50 texts from him today, he wrote:

"Do you really think that with all the resources available to me that I don't know exactly where you have been and what you have done while you were there?"

"Most of us have such a strong tendency to judge and criticize that we can't easily break the habit. However, it's the most important issue to work on immediately. We'll never be able to really love ourselves until we go beyond the need to make life wrong."

-Louise L. Hay

I have really been struggling lately.

I do not have a problem meeting people. I seem to meet and attract people everywhere I go lately—whether it is new friends or men and/or women who want to date me. I feel very fortunate in many ways. I feel very loved by my friends and family.

And *yet*, there is a loneliness in me that I cannot seem to fill.

Lately, I have been feeling that I *really* screwed up my life.

I am starting to feel like I am getting old. I am starting to feel the weight of two divorces. I am starting to feel the consequences of my actions and the decisions I have made. Primarily, the decision to marry my second husband—and then to stay with him for so long when things were so bad.

I am angry at myself for being weak. No one can seem to understand how I got into or stayed in that situation. I suppose that is why I have stayed in familiar territory for so long. I am enjoying meeting new people but I am tired of explaining the *whys* of my life. That said, I feel that the future is in moving forward, not in going back.

It is apparent to me now how much of a mental, physical and emotional drain my ex has been over the last eight years.

"Can you see the possibilities a relationship offers? Explore the possibilities. Be yourself. Find a person who matches with you. Take the risk but the honest. If it works, keep going. If it doesn't work, then do yourself and your partner a favor: walk way; let her go. If it's not going to work, it is better to look in a different direction. If you cannot love your partner the way she is, someone else can love her just as she is. Don't waste your time, and don't waste your partner's time. This is respect."

-Don Miguel Ruiz, *The Mastery of Love*

I was doing a lot of thinking and reading on a camping trip last week. It was very interesting for me to be so up close and personal with another family I have known and admired for 10-15 years.

Ironically, Ricardo—the one who my former father-in-law hassled about our rehearsal dinner—invited me and my children to their annual camp out on Orcas Island. His grandchildren went to Montessori with my kids for years and became close. It was a dream camping trip that I never could have accomplished alone as a single mom. Just being with their wonderful family was healing for all of us.

I think what happened to me growing up is that when my parents divorced, I was labeled as "sensitive" and my family—especially my dad—did everything possible to avoid hurting my feelings or upsetting me. It has been nearly impossible for me to find someone who treats me like my dad did—and I notice with age that my dad does not even treat his own beloved wife that way.

My family is very quiet and kind. We tend to hold things in and let them pass. I think as a result of these things, I don't know how to deal with conflict well or relate to normal family bickering. The slightest thing tends to freak me out—especially after being on the complete opposite side of things with my ex and his family.

My ex father-in-law's wife once told me they were tired of walking on eggshells with me. It angered me at the time, but there was probably some truth in her statement.

I realized on this trip how crucial it is for my kids to have a good father figure in their lives. I have been filling in the blanks the best I can but there are some things that can't be substituted. I don't expect that their dad is ever going to be capable of filling that role. Hopefully they will be OK for the time being with the other good men in our lives.

I spent Sunday night with my first husband and his family. They had an enormous party and I met many new people. Several of them commented on me doing so much for them and I told them, it goes both ways—it always have. There were *so* many times when he and his wife had been there for me over the years. They are both so special to me. There is *nothing* either of them would not do for a friend.

It makes me sad on some level that I did not realize what I had with him way back when. But I do believe everything happens for a reason and I am very grateful to have him and his wife in my life in such a close capacity.

As we were leaving, Hussein kissed my daughter and told her that *he was the reason she had her name*. I don't think she can comprehend our relationship at four, but she does know that we were once married and both of my kids call him *Uncle*.

I have spent some time looking back on all my previous relationships recently and have realized that Hussein is the one who has been there for me through thick and thin. He never chastised me. He never put me down or called me names. He never participated in petty gossip. He was there when both my grandparents died. He wept; hard. My grandparents both loved him as their own, even long after our marriage ended. He remained their grandson, helping them with many things. He has deeply loved all of my family, including my children, as his own. There is something very comforting about knowing that he would be there in a heartbeat if I needed him.

I never had that with my second husband. I only knew drama, heartache and unreliability.

I have learned so much about grace and love through Hussein. It is a relationship that did not remain as we had intended, but it has still been there for both of us all these years. It will always be one of my most fundamental relationships.

I think that many men that I have had relationships with have only seen me as a possession. I was theirs to have and control. When they did not get what they wanted from me, there was always some sort of abuse or mistreatment. I think that is why it has been often easier for me to have lovers than boyfriends. I seem to have more control over my own life that way.

Hussein has never been cruel or childish. He always saw me as a person, and wanted the best thing for *me*, even when at times it was not the best thing for *him*. And I have done the same for him.

That is love.

"I took a deep breath and listened to the old bray of my heart.
I am. I am. I am."

-Sylvia Plath

I feel deeply saddened that me and my children are back to survival mode.

I want to do so much more than just *survive*.

It struck me yesterday just how much I have lost in these last eight years.

My face is worn and tired. I know that beauty is not everything. But, I still wish I had not wasted my best years without sleep, love or proper companionship. And I regret that there was so much pain, tears and solitude.

I want to be able to have a "normal" relationship. And I have not been able to do that even now that I am divorced because so much of my energy is directed at my ex-husband and figuring out how to protect my children.

I want my children to do *more* than survive. I want them to *thrive*. I want them to know joy and laughter; the carefree days of childhood. I want them to laugh, to play and to have fun.

I want to read more. I want to write more. I want to have a fulfilling career. I want to learn how to play the piano and speak other languages. I want to travel.

I want to *live*.

"I don't want to get to the end of my life
and find that I lived just the length of it.
I want to have lived the width of it as well."

-Diane Ackerman

There is a picture somewhere of my Nana and me when I was a little girl. I don't know why this picture always comes to mind for me, but it does.

She was a young grandmother—only 36 when I was born. In this photo, we are both facing their glass sliding glass door toward the backyard.

She's wearing tight 70's bell-bottoms and a sheer, fitted blouse. I cannot see either of our faces—although my Nana was beautiful.

I just remember that we were both looking out that window into her garden—perhaps looking toward better things.

This is what grief feels like... the faraway picture of the dream that never quite arrives.

If you look at your grandmother's picture long enough, it may well break your heart.

While I was caring for my paternal grandma, I found out Nana was also dying. I thought I still had time with her, as she was two decades younger.

A month after Nano's funeral we had our annual family reunion for my mom's side of the family. It was held at the same park down the street from my grandparent's house that they have lived in since my mom was a teenager.

Ironically, my great grandmother was also still alive at nearly 95 years of age. I went to the reunion with a heavy heart knowing it would likely be the last year for both my grandma and my great grandma.

My great grandmother latched on to me each time I hugged her with forceful squeezes. She has never been much of a hugger, so I knew she was thinking the same thing I was. It is difficult for her to hear much of anything anymore—so it's hard to carry on a conversation that doesn't consist of me yelling and her asking, "What? What?" to everything directed at her. The most content she seemed all afternoon was when my cousin's two-year-old sat on her lap and played with her necklaces. No conversation was needed. She sat there and smiled at her and the girl smiled back.

For the most part, it was just nice to sit by her side and know she was still there.

My grandmother's cancer has spread everywhere. It's in her brain and she has an enormous tumor sticking out of her collarbone that is difficult to even look at. She gave in and started some radiation a few weeks ago, as it was the only way to prolong the inevitable. She started to lose her hair yesterday, which was very difficult for her to accept. She has always been a beautiful and well-kept woman. She told me she was going to go out and get a "damned sexy" wig with real hair.

She is keeping a good humor about it all. She does not complain and she hates for anyone to feel sorry for her. She told me she was *lucky.* The bulging tumor could have been on her face or somewhere that was even more obvious.

It is so difficult for me to watch a woman who has always been in motion—who raised five children and many grandchildren—slow down. She was exhausted, but she wanted to do this picnic for our family, like every other year. I was grateful that she has her boyfriend there and my uncle to take care of her every need. They both adore her.

I didn't see my grandmother's boyfriend until about half way through the party. He was busy taking care of everything so my grandmother wouldn't have to. I asked him how he was doing, and he buckled up and said he was holding in there. I looked him in the eye and told him, "Thank you for taking such good care of my grandma." He started to choke up and nearly lost it. We embraced for a very long time.

They have been together for at least 10 years. It took a long time for me to accept him because *no one* is ever going to be my grandpa. However, over the years, I have come to love him and appreciate how much he loves my grandmother. My kids consider him their grandpa. He's what they have known and he's good to them. He's been good to all of us.

I seem to be breaking up over this grandmother more than the death of the other. I suppose I thought her death was natural and her time had come. But I don't feel that way now. It seems her life has been cut so short, and so unfairly. It is a hard thing for me to accept, but I know I will have to soon.

For now, I am just grateful to have the family that I have. I am trying to appreciate the time that I have had with my grandmother and her mother—and spend as much time with them as possible before it is too late.

"Never ever again will I accept that someone else's reality is mine, just to make them happy."

-Kristen Johnston, *Guts*

Nana deteriorated quickly. She had major shoulder pain for months and no one could figure out why. The cancer has eaten through her shoulder bone and so it is essentially broken.

It seems we are just all waiting now for the inevitable to happen. It is sad and painful. I seem to be almost in a daze, getting lost going places that I have been a million times.

Yesterday she was so out of it. Her face had turned gray and my aunt from Texas had decided to put makeup on her. She looked like a ridiculous clown; her bald head covered by a pink hat and black eyebrows painted above her eyes with a smudge of mis-colored rouge over her cheeks.

I preferred seeing her gray. It was better than haphazardly hiding what we all know is about to happen.

My aunt had made turkey that looked under-cooked to me. I didn't say anything but declined to eat. My grandmother wouldn't eat the turkey either. She kept looking at the clock and saying it hadn't cooked long enough. Everyone else was drunk except for my mom and me so they didn't seem to notice. They all acted like my grandma was nuts, but I told her I thought it needed more time too. My uncle had given up feeding her and told me to do it so I transferred most of her food to my mom's plate. She asked me if I could lie. I realized I could—for her.

My Mormon uncle who had been sober almost 20 years started drinking again. I reconnected with my cousin lately but had not realized that we had both married alcoholics. It is crazy that alcoholism is so damned secretive—even in families that should know better. We could have been helping each other all these years. Instead, we both held our shame privately, always pretending that our lives were just so. No wonder her daughter and my son (who are only two weeks apart) had such an instant connection.

It's like a strange destiny we were both pulled toward. All the blame I have been feeling toward myself sort of dissipated when I heard her story. I suppose you are pulled toward what you know.

And in knowing this I realized that all of my family is yanked this direction and so is my ex.

My grandma has been telling me not to get remarried. She keeps telling me not to have more children. She says it urgently, nearly every time I see her. I keep thinking of the Audre Lorde poem, "A Litany for Survival."

> *For those of us who live at the shoreline*
> *standing upon the constant edges of decision*
> *crucial and alone...*

"When you rape, beat, maim, mutilate, burn, bury, and terrorize women, you destroy the essential life energy on the planet. You force what is meant to be open, trusting, nurturing, creative, and alive to be bent, infertile and broken."

-Eve Ensler, *The Vagina Monologues*

Yesterday was one of the worst days of my life.

We skipped church because we all had the beginnings of colds. The morning was peaceful—just hanging out with the kids and not doing much of anything. I made the kids waffles, and actually ate one myself, which I rarely do anymore. It was *really* good.

My uncle called early afternoon and told me to get over as soon as I could. He said to bring the letters and copy of the new will I had helped my grandma with. He said she was *done* and intended to have hospice come in the next hour to assist with death.

I rushed over and found nearly all my aunts and uncles there. Nana was calling other relatives in tears, saying goodbye.

Hospice arrived 20 minutes after me. We were told that nothing would happen until the next day. My grandma started bawling and said she couldn't live like *this* anymore and said she would just get the shotgun or jump off a bridge.

A counselor was brought in and the time frame went to one week —and then to 15 days. Nana explained that she didn't want to keep shitting all over herself and she could no longer do anything that she enjoyed or that made her life worthwhile. It was terrible to see this strong woman reduced to tears and begging.

Meanwhile my aunt and uncle went into the other room to count all the cash money she had saved up all these years, which was more than I would have thought with her small dog grooming business. They divided it by five for each of her children, and later by six to include her long-time boyfriend.

I lay with my grandma in her bed for the last hour before I left. I was crying softly and she noticed. She told me that I would be *OK* and that I would *find a nice man who would love me and my kids*. I realized in that moment that she had full confidence in me and she didn't have the worry for me she did with many of her children. It was a very empowering moment. She didn't leave me with money. She left me with her full trust that I would be alright. That was a greater gift.

I am very angry that she is not able to leave her life with dignity as she had planned. The morals of our country make no sense to me. We have no problem taking the lives of people around the world who are not ready to leave their life or their family. But when one of our own is suffering and ready to go, our "ethics" dictate that they have to wait an arbitrary 15 days.

Fifteen days of additional profit is what it amounts to. Everything in life seems to come back to money.

> "At the end of the day, we can endure much more
> than we think we can."
>
> -Frida Kahlo

I just came from my grandmother's house. She is really out of it now. It is so sad to see her this way. It is good she had some extra meat on her bones to begin with because she is really skinny now.

Her brain is nearly gone. She got confused and told my mom she *needed to leave*. My mom ran out, and we all knew she was upset. I had been there for about an hour before that, so I knew that she was just completely mixed up. I asked her if she wanted me to leave too and she said *yes*. Then she realized what she had done and asked me to run back out and get my mom. She had already left.

The social worker helped me give her a bath. She perked up then, but it was humiliating for her when we washed her private parts and she started to cry. It broke my heart.

I was glad to have someone helping me. She was very kind and it didn't seem as hard as it had with my paternal grandma when I had to do it alone. She kept things light. I will not let myself break down in front of her again.

Nana did not want hospice there again today and she has said that several times now. As it turns out, it *is* a profit thing. My uncle had reiterated to one hospice worker yesterday that she didn't want everyone there and the woman snapped back that he *had* to let them come because if they didn't come, *they wouldn't get paid*.

I have learned a lot about our system of dying in the last three years. This is the third grandparent to use hospice. There is a lot I would change.

It is too late now for the so-called assisted suicide to help us, as my grandma had wanted. She will not make it 15 days. She just has to suffer until her death. All we can do is make her as comfortable as she can be.

Someone called hospice to tell them that they think my uncle will try to help my grandma die. So now, they are *really* watching him.

I had to document and destroy all the meds with the nurse. She had to have me sign that I had witnessed this and helped her dispose of everything. We had to account for every single pill.

She can't swallow anymore so these are all things she cannot even use. Usually they don't do this until someone dies, but because of the call, she thought we should do it then while we were both there.

I could not believe someone did this to my uncle.

He's been there 24-7 for weeks, if not months, and today is probably the last day. He broke down several times. My uncle looks like the Brawny Man. Apart from when his dog died, I don't remember ever seeing him cry.

I had to sit there and defend him, reminding everyone that the bottom line was she didn't want to be like this and she wanted to die more than a week ago.

After the nurse left, I looked at the sexy Glamour Shot of Nana on the wall and thought, *that wasn't so long ago*. You would never know she was the same person, lying there, completely unaware, bald, with her mouth wide open, gurgling.

It is one of the worst things I have ever witnessed to see my Nana like this. It's not like my other grandparents, who were in their nineties. *She still had life yet.*

I had sent our Associate Pastor a picture of her several weeks ago, with her hat to cover her baldness. (She did not want any religious visits, but the women in my church have been continually praying for her.) Then I realized that it did not really show her who she was praying for, so I sent another one of her from a few years ago. She thanked me and said it helped her really recognize our loss.

So there were three people in that room with me—the beautiful grandma I have grown up with, the warrior cancer patient who rose to the occasion, and the corpse lying there—half-dead.

I tried to sing every comforting, non-religious song I could think of and pulled up the "For the Dying" poem that my sister had read to my paternal grandma just prior to her passing. I kept thinking it would be anytime, but she did not pass just then.

"If the world were so organized that everything had to be fair, *no living creature could survive for a day*. The birds would be forbidden to eat worms, and everyone's self-interest would have to be served."
-Wayne Dyer

Nana passed away early this evening surrounded by her family. The cancer took over her entire body.

It seems much to early to be the end of her life. I was born when she was my age. It seems crazy to think of being a grandma now, at only 36.

She was an unconventional, but loving grandma. She was always reading when I was young. The first book she gave me that I remember was Dr. Wayne Dyer's *Your Erroneous Zones*. I think I read it twice, and I had to have been about 13-years-old. The biggest thing it helped me with growing up as a born-again Christian was guilt. I recently saw it on her bookshelf and read it again.

There were so many things like that with her—quiet nudges to prevent us from living painful lives.

She was always beautiful and very smart. I remember hearing my sister's boyfriend (who is in his twenties) remark recently that she was a "damned sexy lady." It was always like that with her.

She taught me a lot about owning my own sexuality as a woman, and never letting society's double standards take hold over me. There was never any nonsense with her, about anything. She never beat around the bush, and I appreciated that about her. That being said, she did not have an unkind bone in her body. I never saw her do anything malicious or mean. If she didn't like something or someone, she was direct about it.

The two sides of my family are very polarized on the surface. My dad's family goes to church and does not ever curse. My Nana was an atheist and cursed like a sailor. I used to cringe at this, but now I appreciate her honesty.

I used to think it was unkind to say words like *Goddamn-it* and *Bitch*, but now I see that it can be just as painful (or more) to remain silent and let the person know passively how pissed off you are. When you say the words, you get it out, and it's over with. When you are silent, the anger remains in the air without the opportunity to address it.

She didn't just praise you just because you were hers—if she did give praise it was sincere and measured. I started making my own body oils a few years ago, and made a special batch for her for Mother's Day last year. She asked me about the ingredients and such and then just said, "Humph!"

A week later she called to tell me that she done an experiment to test my oil against hers. After a week of mine on one arm, she asked her manicurist and a few other people. She was very excited and proud to tell me mine really *was* better!

What I will miss most about Nana is to be able to call her with any cooking question. Neither one of us liked to talk on the phone, but that was one thing we really connected on. She knew the answer to *everything*. She saved many recipes for me.

A few months ago, I had sat out in the sun for too long and then proceeded to try to make two new (and very complicated) appetizers for my friend Bill's German-inspired birthday party. I was so ditsy she asked me, *Are you drunk?* We laughed for a long time about that and I told her that I had not only sat out too long but then proceeded to cut up and empty out 20 jalapeno peppers with my bare hands and every part of me seemed to be *on fire*. Both recipes turned out great despite my missteps.

She was never very emotional or a smothering grandma, but she always made sure you knew how much she loved you. The last months we were together, we almost always sat out on her back deck, until the very end. She always hugged me and told me she *really* loved me. She and my uncle were almost always laughing, even when things were pretty bad for her.

She often surprised me with her thoughtfulness, whether it was calling to check on how a recipe had turned out or worrying about our dog getting trimmed after she became ill.

She loved all of her children so very much, and that was really what stood out to me the most in our last visits together. She was always so concerned about everyone else. When I showed her a wig I had worn at a recent party, she told me she had a perfect bag to go with it and told me to go and get it so I could use it for my Halloween costume.

She, like my other grandparents, always came to all of the parties I threw throughout my 20's and 30's—and there were some crazy ones! She would always join right in and drink whatever we were drinking.

She taught me a lot about taking care of myself and getting lots of exercise. She was moderate in everything and *so* self-sufficient. She believed you had to find your own happiness, and she found hers just being at home, whether cooking or working in her beautiful yard. She was steadfastly *not* religious and I do not believe she ever feared death. The last few days she talked about going to a better place to be with her brother. She never doubted her right to exist in heaven, and neither did I.

We talked many, many times about my marriage and my life. There were a lot of things we both related to. She never told me what to do, but her own life served as an answer for me on many things. In many ways, she had a hard life. But she always seemed content. I will miss her so very much.

I have always felt, when times were hard, that at least I had my family, who is very dear to me. My grandparents in particular have always been a rock for me. Although Nano and Pappa are gone now, I often forget that they are not here. I still feel them very much around me and inside me, and they still buoy me when I would otherwise sink.

I hope that, in time, I will feel this way about Nana too. For now, there is just emptiness and great sadness.

"Return to me. Return to yourself. Remember yourself. Remember me. I am the Great Mother. I am the Goddess. I am the Wise Woman. Listen to my words. Listen to my song. I am in you, thus I can never be lost. My story is your story. And it is the true story of birth and life and death. Eat me. Feed me. You are woman and so am I. Through me, you exist; through you, I exist. We are the ones who create. We are the ones who nourish. We are the ones who open the gates between the worlds. We are the ones who must reclaim ourselves, who must reweave ourselves."

-Susun Weed

I still miss my grandma very much. I momentarily forget that she has passed and then remember sadly that I can't stop by.

One thing that I have been reflecting on lately though is how short life is and how much time we waste.

I regret all the times I was wallowing in my own miserable marriage. I wish I had spent more time with both my grandmothers and my friends.

But more than anything, I regret times arguing with anyone. Arguing is such a draining life-sucker. I don't want to do it anymore. Sometimes you just can't come to terms with someone and the best thing is just to wish them well and move on.

I have spent far too much time in my life trying to make relationships work with people because of the length of our relationship or because they were family.

For the last six years my Nana lived less than 10 minutes away from my house. But I felt like she was my *young and healthy* grandma and I would have at least 20 more years to spend with her.

It occurred to me today that we take life for granted here so much. We assume, like I did, that we are entitled to so much time with our parents or grandparents—but life promises us *nothing*.

At the same time, we are so flip about our policies in this country, which cause the premature death to millions around the world. It is so hypocritical.

I had a thought the other day about dying and our inability to deal with aging.

When we put our elderly away, not only do we deprive them of the life and family they deserve, but also deprive *ourselves*.

I started to think of the grandparents I cared for in the years prior to their death. It was extremely hard in many ways. But one thing that I realized is that I do not fear death or aging anymore the way that many people do.

I have seen things that I would have never thought I could have dealt with. I learned to do so with love and compassion. There were times when I gagged or felt ill at ease, but for the most part, I saw it as an act of caregiving that I was proud to do. These small acts brought me closer to them. Had I not cared for them, we never would have had many of the moments that we did.

When we care for our elders, we enrich our relationship to them and ourselves. We also learn to accept our own aging and eventual death. We see the big picture, and we are all better for it.

I feel very worn. I know these last years have taken a toll on me. However, I would not trade them for anything. Of all the things I have done in my life—aside from raising my children—this is what I am most proud of.

"We have learned that trauma is not just an event that took place sometime in the past; it is also the imprint left by that experience on mind, brain, and body. This imprint has ongoing consequences for how the human organism manages to survive in the present. Trauma results in a fundamental reorganization of the way mind and brain manage perceptions. It changes not only how we think and what we think about, but also our very capacity to think."

-Bessel A. van der Kolk, *The Body Keeps the Score*

I am trying to minimize as much as possible. It seems like I have been throwing stuff out of my house for three years. I'm taking what I hope is the final sweep through before listing the house for sale.

Basically, I am OK with selling anything and everything now. I was more attached to certain items before because I had put so much time and care into picking each item out. But now I am seeing that this behavior kept me from really living my life. I was so obsessed with everything looking just *right*—it was only a distraction from how messy my life was on the inside.

I remember a friend of mine sold everything he owned a few years ago and started completely over. He kept a bed, a chair and a few books. It was startling to go to his new flat with nothing there. But it was quite freeing for him, and I have watched him really evolve in the years that followed.

It seems I am always in a hurry to have everything change, but nothing became this way overnight. I feel that these last years have been an unraveling of all I covered my true self up with— mostly material, petty things. The more I let go, the better I feel.

It is amazing I even survived living with my ex. Just dealing with him now in small doses takes all the life out of me. My back is causing excruciating pain again. My body feels tired and lifeless. It is no wonder I was accomplishing so little during that time. There was no energy left to do anything. Just get by.

Life is so much more than just *getting by*. I wonder how many women are living this same nightmare. It makes me feel very sad for all of us.

I have much to do now, so there is no time to dwell. But it saddens me that still after all this time, and so many positive changes in my own life, that this one person has the power to suck so much energy from all three of us.

I hope that one day, soon, this will no longer be the case.

> "Self-nurturing requires an attitude of feminine valuing. It is enhanced by the time in which you shift your attention to yourself. If you nurture yourself, the choices you make in your life will be conscious and empowered."
>
> -Virginia Beane Rutter, *Celebrating Girls*

My recent pain has reminded me of some of the choices I have made these last years regarding self-care.

During my marriage, I got chiropractic care, massage and acupuncture regularly.

It has been very clear to me how much stress living (or just dealing) with an addict has put on my body.

Things are much better now, but for years I had chronic headaches, back/neck pain, every sort of stomach issue, and was severely underweight.

I don't have much money now, but one thing I will not scrimp on is my personal care. I say this because I see so many women put themselves last and say, "I can't afford self-care."

I don't believe this is true.

I have had to re-shuffle my priorities, but I am managing.

I did that by canceling cable, eating out less, and basically cutting out little by little anything that was not essential. (Self-care *is* essential!)

I also learned how to do things for myself: like a daily full-body massage—and fire cupping on my back.

I have also been selling things off slowly. I never thought I could (or would) part with many of my possessions, but I feel lighter and happier than I ever have.

What use are diamonds and money to me when I am dead?

I have seen so many women die of cancer after a lifetime commitment to an addict.

I firmly believe that we must take care of ourselves before the addict eats up what's left of us.

Even if you leave, the consequences of living with an addict will hang on for a while. And the effects on your body will remain if you don't deal with them aggressively.

I am sickened to think of all the money wasted on alcohol, drugs, rehabs and recklessness by the addict in my life.

Certainly I am worth the care I need.

"God/dess grant me the compassion to love others the way they are, the wisdom to know when it's abusive or beneficial, and the courage to address it or leave if they persist."

-James Glines

You will never find peace living with an addict. If you try to "help" them, no matter how good your intentions may be, they will only pull you down into their own deep, dark hole. And it will take a *long* time for you to even figure out what happened.

The only solution is to let the addict figure things out for themselves and get help when they are ready.

That may sound harsh, but it's true.

I have finally found peace in my life and I am grateful for that. The only way to maintain it is to have as little contact with him as possible. While this is difficult since we have children together, I can only advise others to limit contact only to what is absolutely necessary. An addict will only drain your time and energy.

At one point, my ex sent me a text telling me I needed to get over my unresolved anger issues. My friend read it and said, "Yes, as long as he continues to do the same things, you have *unresolved* issues."

What I am taking away from this is that I always have a choice. I don't have to engage with my ex or his father. I don't really need to have much to do with either anymore. I can't control their actions, and I think there will always be some amount of craziness involved in the choices my ex makes. So I have to stop believing he can ever be a different person than who he has showed himself to be. And I have to just take responsibility for what I can control—which is me, and the choices I make.

"My grandfather used to tell me that life was a dream. He also said that when people finally realized this, the dream could be changed, and then humanity would change."

-Don Miguel Ruiz

My mom left me when I was four.

At least that's the story I told myself most of my life. It was the story that I had been told and it was the story I identified with, whether it was true or not.

The last memories I have of being close to my mom are from when I was four. I have cherished the pictures of us together, before the divorce.

It's not that I did not love my mom after that. Quite the opposite. I remember clearly lying in my bed alone at night, crying my eyes out when my dad and stepmom thought I was asleep. I was crying for my mother. All I wanted was my mom. In those moments, I told myself she did not love me enough to take me with her.

I felt invisible around my dad. In fact I still do. I know he loves me, deeply. But I don't feel like he has ever really *seen* me. He doesn't *know* me.

I was his loyal little girl for most of my life, well into adulthood. I wanted to please him, and oftentimes, I felt like pleasing my dad included showing disapproval toward my mom. Not that he ever said that, per se. Quite the opposite; I have never heard my dad badmouth anyone.

My stepmother was often abusive. It took a long time for me to finally say that. For most of my life, I have tried to frame everything positively, even when it was not. My sister got most of her wrath because she was spunkier than me. I kept everything inside; I was easier to control.

There are not a lot of moments that stand out to me from my childhood. But I do remember one day in particular with my stepmom when I was 12. We were in the supermarket. I had been going on and on about my "real mom" until her annoyance-level became unbearable. She turned to me and stopped me mid-sentence, hissing with venom: "Your mother is a whore."

I cried my eyes out. I remember sitting in the car with her afterwards, unable to calm down and stop the heaving tears. That statement stung more than any words I had ever heard in my life. To this day, they still cut deep into my heart.

My mother married when she was barely out of high school. To be brief, she ended up having an affair after years of living with my emotionally unavailable father. When he found out, it was painful and dramatic. He never showed her his love, but I remember walking in on him several times as he was crying over my mother. He wrote it all out in music that she never heard until years later. Those images stayed in my mind whenever I dared to side with my mother.

Somewhere in my mid-thirties, I was supposed to go to my father's birthday party. I got a migraine that morning, as I often do when I am avoiding something. And I decided for one of the first times in my life that I would *not* go to his party. Soon after that, I rallied.

Since I rarely have a night without children, I decided to go out with my mother instead. My mom has been my only babysitter all these years, so this was the first time we had ever done this. *We had a blast.* We ate dinner at a local pub, went to see a funny movie, and were headed home when I said, "Mom, how often do we have a chance like this? Let's go do Karaoke!"

My mother, who rarely drinks, had a few cocktails with me and we sang our hearts out. We even danced. I can never remember dancing with my mother—ever. It's a night I will always cherish. It got me thinking: we all ought to have an opportunity to dance with our mothers—at least once, if not often—before we die. On the way home, we talked. We rarely *really* talk. We talk about the kids, and we talk about work, but we rarely talk about what is really going on for both of us.

She mentioned that she was sorry for being a supermom and trying to do it all. And I told her that was never a problem for me. For me it was something else. And I started thinking about the difficulties of mothers and daughters. Longing to be close, but remaining distant for whatever reason. Feeling sorry for things that never bothered the other person at all, and not realizing the things we had both done to hurt each other.

We have a long history in our family of difficult mother-daughter relations, going back at least as far as my great grandmother. There is some sort of legacy there. It is time to break traditions of hurt and heal together.

I had recently submitted an article to be published anonymously that I had written years ago. And in that article I had written that I did not have the close relationship with my mother that I yearned for. I realized, gratefully, during our talk that that was no longer the case.

It was first time I told my mom she was a great mother, and I meant it.

Just before my daughter was born, I had a freak out moment with my mom. My first pregnancy was with a son, which jolted me into action—and therapy. I knew I had things to work on before I could become a mother. I was terrified to have a daughter and very happy when I learned I would have a boy first. I always knew I would have a daughter too.

Late into my pregnancy, I wrote my mother a lengthy letter filled with all my grievances. She sent me one back. Even my sister got in on it. Things were tense for many months, and then we all just made up.

It's not important what was said anymore. *I'm over it.* Being a mother has both healed the old wounds and made me have more grace and understanding toward my mother. It has also caused me to reflect on how I have behaved as a daughter.

In a memoir co-written with her mother, Mia Fontaine wrote:

> "The world is full of instructions and advice on how to mother, in bookstores, in academia, on the playgrounds, in the media. Mothers are always examining how they treat their children, but aside from the occasional 'Don't talk to your mother that way,' or 'You shouldn't have listened to your mother,' there's not much guidance out there for daughters." -Mia Fontaine, *Have Mother, Will Travel*

In the Western world, we often have an unspoken contract with our mothers. We have extremely high expectations. We expect them to be beautiful, perfect and forever at our disposal. While we submit to the father authority, we often treat our mothers as our slaves. We do not allow them to be fully themselves. We expect them to be *our mothers*. We are often unable to see the bigger context of their lives.

We perpetuate our mothers' oppression by following patriarchal patterns and in doing so, we perpetuate our own oppression. Perhaps no other relationship on earth has such blurry lines of separation. *Do we ever fully separate from our mothers?* Our identities are so strongly bonded to theirs, even when we are estranged.

The most primal need of most of us is to be loved by our mothers. Nothing is more painful or more devastating to feel that love cut off. In my case, it was the stories I told myself that did the most damage. As I look back as an adult woman and mother, I know that my mom did the best she could. She gave all she had. She loved me enormously.

My mother was also a victim of a patriarchal system that I supported for most of my life. For that, I am truly sorry.

The separation many women experience with their mothers prohibits them from living full lives. The fact is that women cannot do it all. Perhaps my mother's apology about trying to be superwoman was more about that than anything else. Perhaps I could not hear her words. Perhaps we are socialized to discredit and not listen to our mothers. Coming together as partners is how I see modern motherhood working. Taking from both east and west—giving and receiving.

As I walked hand-in-hand with my daughter to school earlier this week, I started thinking. I was struck with gratitude and a realization that the most painful thing in the world for me would be to be separated from my children. Knowing the way my mother loves, I finally caught a glimpse of her pain. Looking back at the times that we were together, it is her small acts of kindness that always get to me. The way she made my peanut butter sandwiches with a chocolate chips in the middle shaped like a heart. Her little notes in or on my lunch bag. The way she made me feel like I was the most precious creature in the world.

For a long time, I don't think I let myself feel the depth of her love for me.

For more than a year we worked together on my first book, *The Girl God.* It was more work than I ever could have imagined. I never could have done it without my mom. She helped with editing, website, design—you name it. I had to rely on my mother more than I did since I was a child, and at times that was very uncomfortable for me. I had to learn how to accept help, which I have just never done well.

My entire spirituality evolved in the process. I wrote the book for my daughter, but it has also been healing for me. Oftentimes as women, we don't do things for *ourselves*. We will do anything for our children, but we usually come in last.

I never would have written that book for myself.

I wrote it because I knew that things had to change for my daughter, and that soon evolved into realizing that things need to change for the entire world. And finally, I came to recognize that things also need to change for *me*—and the way I value myself as a woman.

I had known that intellectually since discovering feminism nearly 20 years ago. But it was not until I embraced Goddess, that I actually *felt* it.

Since I come from a Fundamentalist Christian background, the idea of a "Girl God" was foreign to both my mother and me. I venture to say that this is not a project she would have been interested in either, if it were not for my longing to complete it. We had both been cut off from the idea of a Mother God. I often wonder how that has affected our relationship.

My daughter identified the Girl God with the image of my mother as her grandma. Seeing our mothers through children's eyes is a refreshing lens. I now also see the Divine in my mother. It's as if it was there all along, but I had not recognized it.

My mother's strong arms give the best hugs. How comforting it would have been to feel the arms of the Goddess around me as a child. It saddens me to think both She—and my mother—were there all along.

Now that I am finally able to feel the love from both of them, I am healing. I have begun to tell a different story about my mother. It is a story that will perhaps always be evolving; however, it seems more accurate and balanced with time.

I had the most beautiful mother in the world. She was *magical.* She read me stories every night, made the best homemade food and gave me all her love. For a time we were separated. We both grew up; we grew stronger. We did the things we had to do. And, then we came together, forgave each other—and changed the world together, hand-in-hand.

Goddess of My Own Damned Life

"Happiness is a spiritual value."

-Z. Budapest

I realized today that I feel happier than I have probably ever felt.

This is something I have been working on for a long time: *just to be happy.*

For some people it probably seems like a simple thing. But for me, it has not been.

I had so many negative thoughts constantly popping into my head that I think I needed to completely re-arrange the way I thought. For me, listening to meditations and other positive, affirming voices really helped.

I've been listening to Patricia Lynn Reilly's *Home is Always Waiting* Meditation (which is wonderful!) every night when I put my daughter to sleep. Sometimes she wants to just talk to me, and that is OK. But I think we both benefit from Patricia's words and her peaceful voice. Throughout the day, beginning with breakfast, I listen to Chakra meditations. This is an area of work my sister has encouraged in me for years. It was only recently that this did not seem "weird" to me.

I have been walking my hilly neighborhood daily and following up with my Kundalini Yoga DVD afterwards. The walking helps me clear my head so I can really experience the yoga. When I tried to do yoga just by itself, I would often get distracted with thoughts or things to do mid-way through.

I was really hard on myself for not doing the yoga and walking daily, but when I let go of that and just decided to do what I could, I started to really enjoy it—and make it a priority every day.

I also decided to make myself a nice salad every day at lunch. In the past, I only made salads when *other people* were eating with me. Now I've figured out a method to make a nice single salad—the way I like with lemon and olive oil—without it being too much fuss. I actually enjoy putting it all together.

I have more time for me now. Part of this is that both my children are in school all day now. I never had time to do all these self-care acts. I have never had a live-in *partner*. And I never demanded partnership. I think in a lot of ways I felt lucky just to have the "privilege" of being married. Contrary to what Al-Anon promotes, I don't think you can be happy or healthy in a toxic environment. I don't believe children can be either.

Now that I am healing myself, I have more creative energy than I have ever had. I have so many projects that I am working on and am excited about. Previously, everything looked good on the outside, but I was a miserable mess. Now, by all accounts, I should probably be miserable—*at least by my old value system*. But I am really, really happy.

"Love comes when manipulation stops; when you think more about the other person than about his or her reactions to you. When you dare to reveal yourself fully. When you dare to be vulnerable."

-Dr Joyce Brothers

It is possible to have a loving and peaceful relationship. When there is constant arguing and drama, it is a sign that the relationship is not right.

It is possible to be in a relationship without arguing all the time. It is possible to have a disagreement and handle it peacefully and lovingly. It is possible to be completely wide-open with someone and not have him use it against you later.

These things may seem obvious, but they were totally out of my radar when I was in relationship with my ex. It was so off-balance and dysfunctional that I completely lost my grounding. My only really strong example of love in my life was my paternal grandparents, who were happily married for 64 years. I think if I had not had that example, I would never have found my way back to a good relationship. They were my guiding stars, and I believe they sent me an angel in the form of the man I am with now.

I have found love.

Sometimes it takes a few relationships that *don't* work to realize what you *do* want.

When I was going through my certification process with *Imagine a Woman*, there was a segment on relationships. I think it was one of the best things I have ever seen on relationships. It was such a moment of clarity for me, and it was so simple—just noticing how you felt in someone's presence.

"Noticing Feelings[6]

After each encounter with a new friend or potential lover, ask yourself:

1. "How did I feel in his/her presence?"
Underline or highlight the words that best describe your feelings.
"I felt _____ in his/her presence today."

excited
turned on
challenged
opened
energized
---
fearful
restrained
cautious
on guard
misunderstood

For the first time, I feel only what is in the top section. In my past relationships, it was usually a mix of both—or in the case of my addict-ex-husband, it was only the bottom portion of the list.

Sometimes as women I think it's very difficult for us to give up even a very bad relationship. It is ingrained in us from childhood that a relationship is the primary thing that gives us value. When we realign with our feelings, we know what is right for us when it comes.

_____

[6] Reilly, Patricia Lynn. Imagine a Woman Empowerment Program, Fundamentals VI "Relationships From the Inside Out." Imagine a Woman International. The full list of feelings is available in this course, which I highly recommend.

> "Rock bottom became a solid foundation upon
> which I built my life."
> -J.K. Rowling

Before I met my love, I had given up on men. Divorced twice with two kids, I didn't feel like I had it in me. I had dated some, the longest relationship lasting six months to a man I later realized I was completely incompatible with. He was just *so* much better than my ex-husband that it seemed like a devastating loss at the time. The once-a-week slot I had available for dating didn't cut it for him.

I had some fun, in the limited ways single moms *can* have fun. I engaged in a relationship with a woman, which was fabulous. It opened me up to myself in ways relationships with men had not. I briefly considered whether I was, in fact, a lesbian. In looking back, I think I could have gone either way. But in this period of grief, longing, experimentation and reflection, I began to compose a list.

The list was everything I wanted in a *man*, so I suppose a man is what I got. It contained roughly 45 things I required in a man: not homophobic, likes sex, not obsessed with money, no texting while he's with me...

Like everyone else in the world, a friend had talked me into the wonders of Facebook. I began accumulating friends. I had a policy, which was to accept everybody. Over the years, I have only had to de-friend a few people. Most people are wonderful additions to my life. In doing so, I never really did that much background checking on the people who friended me. I just clicked "accept" and sporadically read what later came up on my feed.

On my son's eighth birthday, I received a brief message from a man named Anders, and for whatever reason, I looked at his picture. He was *cute*.

I sent him a message back, and with the gaiety of the day, told him I thought he was *very handsome*. This resulted in some back and forth between us. I started looking through his pictures and his posts. I liked what I saw. Within four days, I had purchased a camera for my computer. With a little online help from him, I set it up in under an hour.

We talked for eight hours straight the first time, with bathroom breaks, until my mother came home with my children. We started talking endlessly about everything daily. He possessed every single attribute on my list, but, he lived in Norway with his kids. I lived in Portland with my kids and my ex would never budge on an international move.

Many people thought I was crazy. My ex asked me why I had chosen the furthest possible place away and was not at all sympathetic to our plight. "It's not my fault you chose a guy in *Norway*. Why don't you find someone here in town?"

For me it wasn't that simple. I never had found exactly what I was looking for in *anyone*. I had found shades of *better*, but that wasn't what I wanted. I did not want to *settle*. In fact, I had been perfectly content to just give up on a relationships until my kids grew older. I had just told a close friend that I didn't think I was meant to be in a long-term relationship. He reassured me that I shouldn't hold myself up to anyone else's standards.

Anders was all the things I never thought I could find all at once. He was kind *and* sexy, both masculine *and* a feminist. Within a week, we decided we wanted to be "in a relationship." Shortly thereafter, we decided we would marry. A well-meaning friend asked me about chemistry. She said she'd met men before through the Internet, and it was magical, but once they met in *person* it all fell flat.

With Skype, I somehow felt it was different. We *had* been intimate, perhaps more intimate than many couples are in person. We often talked about how it would be when we met—how long would we wait until we ripped each other's clothes off. In most of the narratives, we made it as far as the airport parking lot.

When we met, three months later, there was a slight awkwardness at the airport. His flight was late. I got on the phone with a girlfriend and chatted nervously. I had bought a dress to wear, but hadn't bothered to try it on first in my excitement. Men and women were eyeing me in a way I wasn't accustomed to.

My breasts were spilling out the top. The hemline was shorter than anything I'd worn since college. And to top it off, I had decided to wear wedge sandals with a five-inch heel. When I had worn them with jeans they seemed fine. But with the mini dress, I looked like a ridiculous woman nearing 40 who was trying to look 15.

Every time a bald-headed man walked out of customs, I scrutinized him to see if it could possibly be Anders. Once I saw him, there was no mistake. His smile caught my gaze and I walked toward him. There was some awkwardness in our hug. I was nearly as tall as him with the heels on, and we didn't align quite right. I wished I could put my regular mommy flats back on.

He also felt uncomfortable. He had worn a long shirt and a jacket on the flight. It was a very warm July in Portland. When we got to the car, instead of me climbing on his lap as we had imagined, he opened his suitcase and searched frantically for a shirt to wear. He couldn't find what he thought he had brought. There was only a sort of European "wife-beater" tank top. He removed his shirt in the parking lot and put that on. We embraced once more and got into my Suburban.

We decided to take our time and take the long way home, which I was grateful for. We were chatting, but my mind was busy. I felt nervous and sweaty. Then he took my hand, and it all felt *right*.

When we got home, I offered him a glass of water and that was all it took to break the ice. We melted into each other perfectly and every awkwardness was gone.

For about a year, we took turns visiting each other. Skype supplemented our visits. We talked every day for hours. While I wished I could have the luxury of living with him in person, it was by far the best relationship I have ever been in.

For a long time, I was just floating along with my life. I did things almost always by accident, or whatever came along. I was a Christian and a "good girl" because that's what my family expected. I went to college because I was supposed to. I got married too young because I didn't want to be living in "sin." I got pregnant by accident. I got married again because I wanted to be a good girl *again*.

As I've gotten older, I have started to live more intentionally. I may be broke, but for the first time, I am really living for me, not a paycheck, a diamond or a man. I love Anders, but I don't *live* for him. Part of the beauty of being apart is that we have our own lives and we are present when we are together. But I miss him desperately when he leaves. The first days are always the hardest. It's difficult to describe the longing I feel. It is both the wistfulness of a young girl in love and the regret of an older woman who continuously kicks herself for her previous life choices.

Once you have children, there are things you can't undo. You are stuck not only with the ex-spouse, but also with the problems the children have inherited from them. When you are dealing with an addict who has relapsed more times than you care to count, you have to always be on guard. You don't carry a child for nine months to let them be carelessly destroyed. You lose your lightheartedness about life. You can't plan ahead. When you make plans for trips, they are often cancelled at the last minute. When you have dreams you want to pursue, they are at the constant whim of being the sole care-giver for your children.

So here you are in this great new relationship feeling better than you have since you can remember but you still have all this residue. Not from yourself, because you worked on *that* for years and years. But you still have an ex who comes and takes all the outdoor furniture while you are out with your new boyfriend. Or he refuses to bring the kids home when he's supposed to and you have to call the police because you think he might be driving around with them drunk. Or he starts yelling at you in front of your boyfriend and while you want to scream back, you also don't want to seem like a crazy person.

And with most men, you would either have to hide or downplay all of this because you have been a perfectionist all your life and you think no one could possibly take all this in. And then you realize, *this* is intimacy. You finally have exposed *all* of your life to someone and he loves you anyway.

> "Own who you are but know that who you are
> can always change."
>
> -Julie Powell, *Lessons from Julia Child*

My reformation from country club princess to granola mama didn't happen all at once. It began when I turned off my TV and woke the fuck up.

I had been slowly evolving for a while, but things changed drastically for me when I met Anders and experienced his culture in Norway.

As with most travel and exposure to other cultures, it's what I noticed about what we took for granted as "normal" here that opened my eyes the most.

It delights me that there are natural-looking women on the front of Norwegian magazines, complete with wrinkles and double chins. I love the way there's a healthy medium on the weight issue —you rarely see someone who is either anorexic or obese. I relish the fact that it's highly unusual to see a homeless person.

I didn't realize how badly we denigrated those who don't drive cars here in the U.S. until I re-watched *The 40-Year-Old Virgin* with Anders. While I still find that movie hysterical, it is interesting social commentary that the nerdy virgin rides a bike.

Anders noticed it right off the bat. "Men who don't drive cars here are really treated like losers aren't they?"

I realized he was right. How many times are people completely identified with their cars? How many times has a woman turned down a nice guy because she didn't like his car? And how do men complete the role of "man" if they cannot pick up a woman for a date?

My ex said the same thing to me in the beginning. He laughed about Anders driving around in one of his velomobiles, careful like most of those in "polite" society not to say anything directly offensive. It amounted to this: how strange that a [real] man wouldn't have a car!

Let's be honest: *It does seem weird*. We take it for granted in this country that people own cars. And the richer they are, the nicer that car should be.

Women have diamond wedding rings and purses, but men really just have their cars to advertise their worth. And the owning part of that usually means they have financed a car—or rather, that they're indebted to someone else for their sense of self.

On my first trip to Norway, it was wet and rainy every day. We traveled by foot, bus or train. Every excursion required that we walk at least 10 minutes up or down a steep hill. I saw many people of all ages walking up and down the hill all day long, many carrying heavy bags of groceries. When we shopped, we carried our own groceries back.

It wasn't so bad. I got used to the rain and the exercise felt good throughout the day. The elderly were not isolated—in fact, there were some pretty old people who seemed a lot more fit than most of the teenagers I see in America. And, I noticed that nearly no one was overweight.

I am someone who has always believed you had to have a car. My ex-husband was actually a high-end car dealer for most of our marriage. I had driven a large Suburban around guiltily for years. When I bought it, I planned to have a bunch more kids. That obviously never happened. I still drove the car around anyway, saying it was nice to have when we had other kids in the car... which was practically never.

Seeing how people lived in Norway was the first time I actually stopped and thought about why having a car was necessary. But I had one excuse left: my kids.

During their primary years, my children attended private school, which required that I drive 45 minutes each way, twice a day. In addition to wasting three hours a day driving, I was spending an enormous amount on gas. I hated the commute and the fact that I was wasting so much fuel, but I was sold on the idea of private school. I sacrificed much of what I would have been entitled to in the divorce so that my kids could attend that school.

The reason we left the private school is a whole separate book—but we did leave and I have no regrets.

Eventually, I decided to sell my car. It was a hysterical process for a woman who had never sold a car by herself and did not want to ask her ex-husband for help. After nearly six weeks with the same buyer, I finally sold the car.

In the suburban community I previously lived in, it would have been nearly impossible to live without a car. I eased into it. I still had my long commute for a period, but I managed to car-share with my mother and make it work with a somewhat crazy schedule. I had a car approximately four days a week, and made sure to do my errands on those days.

During the transition, I got used to walking more. In the suburbs, when you walk, people assume you must be having car problems. I can't tell you how many times a friend stopped, worried that my car had broken down. While I appreciated the sentiment, I found it quite amusing!

I decided to move back to a flatter, more urban part of Portland where I could walk nearly everywhere. I sold more than half my belongings and moved into a smaller space we shared with another family for the next eight months. I found the local public school to be more than acceptable.

We walk or bike to and from school every day, stopping on the way home for groceries. Obviously, the summer months are better weather-wise. It's sunny and beautiful in the summer in Portland. The fall, winter and spring months are notoriously rainy and wet.

Americans spend an average of 75 minutes a day in their cars.

I always hated driving. It made me tired and cranky to sit in traffic. I now spend an average of 75 minutes a day walking, which means I'm in fairly good shape without a gym membership.

Life has become extraordinarily simple. If I need something, I walk to get it. Oftentimes, I end up deciding I don't really need what I thought I did, after I weigh in on how to get there. I finally know my neighbors and the people in my community.

If I need to go somewhere distant, I usually take a bus. Public transportation in Portland is great once you learn the schedules. On some occasions, I use a Zipcar, but that's more and more uncommon. I usually only need to use a car once a month, due to a holiday or celebration. The last time I took a car was on Eid ul-Adha for a party far across town.

On the way home, I reflected on how cars separate people from each other. When you're walking, you greet people face-to-face. When you're in your car, you rarely look at the other drivers. You look at their cars. You feel isolated and oddly protected.

This got me thinking about the other big difference I noticed about driving in Norway. With nearly a zero tolerance policy for any alcohol in the system, I never once have seen someone drink and drive. In the U.S., people tend to push the limits, saying, "I've only had one or two drinks." I often see people leave parties clearly intoxicated, while their "friends" just wave them off like there's nothing wrong with that.

I think our cars make us think we're safe. And they separate us from the people that we might hit or even kill. We become reckless, whether by using our cell phones while driving or taking a drink before we drive.

We have become an extremely disconnected society.

I realized on that last drive that I didn't miss having a car. I don't have insurance, car payments or gas and maintenance expenses. I'm in a good mood from all the daily exercise I get. I don't plan to ever own a car again. Why should I?

I know many people will find the thought of not owning a car practically insane. But consider this: *Driving a car is the most air polluting act an average citizen commits.*

I've heard many mothers say that the best conversations they have with their children is when they're in the car. I have one problem with that: you have your back turned to your child and your eyes on the road. What happened to talking face-to-face? There's something magical about walking side-by-side with someone and really talking.

The other day, I stopped at the store and bought more than usual. Walking back with 50 pounds of groceries in the pouring rain with my daughter caused me to reflect on something else. I realized that some people probably saw us walking in the rain and felt sorry for us. But we were laughing. We have at least half an hour a day to walk side-by-side, talking about what matters to us.
Of all the reasons I love not having a car, that daily experience tops the list.

If you look at my life through the lens of what I'm supposed to have, *I shouldn't be happy.*

I have a lot of gray hair. I don't wear a tiny size anymore—or belong to a country club or even a gym. I'm twice divorced. I don't have a "job." I don't have a car... the list goes on and on.

I realize that I am fortunate. I chose to give those things up. As someone who has lived both ways, I have to say that those who don't have the "proper" list of acquisitions are not missing much, if anything.

When I look at my life through my own lens of where I have come from and who I want to be, I'm *thrilled* with where I am at.

"It is important to give yourself credit for all your successes, no matter how small. If you wait to get to the end of the healing process, until you're 'finished,' before you recognize your progress, you'll wait forever. Each small step is a building block, and accomplishment in and of itself, and by acknowledging each step along the way you make room for further growth."

-Laura Davis, *Courage to Heal*

Today is my sort-of wedding day. My ex will not allow my children to come to Norway for our actual wedding, so we are spending the day celebrating in Portland with our four children.

My daughter is thrilled to wear her flower girl dress and ride around in a limo for the first time. We will be joined by my parents later for cake and sparkling drinks. It will be a *happy* day, despite the selfishness of my ex. But I think my children and I will always remember that my ex would not allow them to attend the *actual* ceremony in Norway.

Later I will travel to Norway to meet my husband for our wedding on a Goddess Island. We will travel on a restored sailboat with about 20 friends to experience a shamanic ceremony performed by his best friend.

I will end up crying because, while it is a joyous day, it is rainy day —and none of my friends or family from the U.S. will be able to join us.

During the ceremony, two of his healer friends will do extensive work on both of us. We will let go of the prior pain in our lives while we are underground with our animal spirit helpers. We will be encircled by our friends—and Anders' family—who love us and want the best for our life together. There will be rattles and drums and storytelling from the journeys our guests had while they were underground.

Afterwards, we will sail back to the mainland and eat a hearty meal complimented by wine, singing and dancing.

In the end, the day will be a bit *too* much for me and the tears will flow. The release from those tears will start a healing process that will change my life forever.

"Pretty is a tyrant who requires costumes, masks, and procedures in exchange for a compliment. Pretty is a junkie who sells us our fix each morning and stalks us all day with a mirror. Pretty is a distraction who keeps us occupied so we don't make a fuss, start a movement, change the world. Pretty is make believe. Say NO to pretty!"

-Patricia Lynn Reilly

A few years ago, my "gay husband," Salvador, came over for a long afternoon visit that stretched into dinner with my actual husband, Anders.

My actual husband never had the opportunity to meet my grandparents, which is a real shame. I know they would have loved him. And he would have felt right at home with them. I took the opportunity to have Salvador tell Anders about who they were as people from his perspective.

Salvador spoke about how loving my grandparents were—with us and with each other. My dad's parents were married for nearly 65 years. They are my only real example of what a good marriage can look like over time.

Something came out that was rather enlightening for me.

Salvador said my grandpa always saw me as his *very* little girl, no matter how old I got. When he said that, it clicked for me in a way that made me realize it was true.

To both my grandparents, I was always their "Princess."

My eagerness for that title prompted me to be the good little girl who always did what was expected of me.

Salvador went on to say that gorgeous women always have the same problem. We're primped to be beautiful at the expense of all else and then agonize over why the man of the moment does not love us. "It has to go *both* ways honey!" he laughed.

I realized then what my problem had been my entire life.

When we grow up believing in the princess fallacy, we actually believe that if we play by all the good princess rules, that life will work out for us, as we want it to. Thus, we're baffled when men don't respond to us.

Few men actually want a caricature—at least not long-term.

Being a princess means that you don't ever dare go outside the princess box. Princesses don't have their periods. They don't talk about any sort of discomfort, let alone the bloody messes. They don't get raped, they don't get molested, and they don't get depressed. They certainly don't throw temper tantrums. In short, princesses always have to appear perfect. They don't go out without being dressed properly with their makeup-mask on and hair done just so. If our lives *look* perfect, *we* must be, *right*?

Being a princess meant that I was never really fully myself around my family. We didn't talk about my highest aspirations or very lowest moments. We didn't talk about theirs either. *Princesses cannot be bothered with all of that.*

It was only on the day my grandmother died that I found out she had been married briefly before she met my grandfather. She had been ashamed, also.

Years later, I still mourn that distance between us. I was finalizing my second divorce when she died. Learning more about her "failures" in life would have helped me tremendously. Hearing about that part of her life allowed me to imagine her off her pedestal. It made me feel closer to my grandma.

Being a princess separates you from other women. Other females are always the competition, because one princess is always prettier than the other. Women who are princesses don't often have women friends—at least close ones. It's just a perpetual beauty contest, where money, "charm" and nice clothes are the only things that count.

It's a contest that no one can win and that *all* women will fail at sooner or later.

I remember being told I was "too pretty to work." So on some level, I always held on to that and resented working when I had to. I resented it every time a man did not pick up the check. It was not part of the unspoken agreement of how a princess *should* be treated.

It also meant that any man who *would* treat me as an equal was off the table for most of my life.

Being a princess meant I didn't know how to live without an enormous household budget or a huge diamond ring. *Wasn't that the ultimate goal*? Did it matter that my ex-husband was an alcoholic and didn't come home at all when he wasn't so inclined?

When I look back at the years of my life when I was playing this role, they were completely non-productive. *Perhaps*, I made a good income; *perhaps* I was a good mother. *Perhaps* I was at my most beautiful. But in terms of creativity and personal fulfillment, there was zilch.

I was only living the life I was *supposed* to be living, not examining what I wanted for myself.

Several years ago, I saw Katie Makkai's transformative poem, "Pretty" performed on You Tube. These lines stuck in my head for years:

"This is about the self-mutilating circus we have painted ourselves clowns in. About women who will prowl 30 stores in six malls to find the right cocktail dress, but haven't a clue where to find fulfillment or how wear joy, wandering through life shackled to a shopping bag, beneath those two pretty syllables."

Being "gorgeous" has more to do with dolling yourself up than actually being beautiful.

At least in how other people perceive you. I am the same woman I have always been, but I noticed when I stopped wearing much makeup or spending time on my hair, people started responding to me differently. I don't get the same over-the-top compliments I used to get, although I must say, I don't *need* to anymore.

My "beauty" has depended a lot on how much time I was spending on primping. Therefore, my theory is we punish women verbally for not "taking care of themselves."

This process robs women of actually doing the things they love. How many times have you seen a woman not get into a swimming pool because a) she didn't want to ruin her hair or, b) she was uncomfortable with her body?

How many times does this happen to a man?

When I look back at pictures of myself wearing a lot of makeup, I feel *angry*. I know those wasted hours could have been better spent. I was hiding behind something: a mask that kept me from achieving my full potential.

That seemed okay for a time because all the compliments made up for it. I was *pretty*. But I cannot make up those lost hours now. The pictures that were once proof of my worth are now painful to look at.

When you fit yourself inside of the pretty box by achieving the ideal weight, the perfectly flattened, colored and styled hair, the right makeup, and the smallest-sized designer clothes—it's supposed to feel *good*. It is supposed to be flattering when people constantly tell you that you have attained this perfect look that females are taught to strive for their entire lives. But the truth is it is *exhausting*. Not only do you spend hours every day to achieve this "effortlessly," but men try to fuck you *from every direction.*

It has been more than 20 years since I read *The Beauty Myth*, but what has *changed*?

> "The more legal and material hindrances women have broken through, the more strictly and heavily and cruelly images of female beauty have come to weigh upon us... During the past decade, women breached the power structure; meanwhile, eating disorders rose exponentially and cosmetic surgery became the fastest-growing specialty... Pornography became the main media category, ahead of legitimate films and records combined, and thirty-three thousand American women told researchers that they would rather lose ten to fifteen pounds than achieve any other goal...More women have more money and power and scope and legal recognition than we have ever had before; but in terms of how we feel about ourselves physically, we may actually be worse off than our unliberated grandmothers."
> -Naomi Wolf (1991)

It seems that our daughters are under even more pressure to conform that we were.

What will it take for women to reject the beauty standards that are holding us back?

Over the last three to four years, my values have changed dramatically. I had to cut back—drastically. In doing so, I have more time for creativity. I went back to my habit of reading several books a week and writing. Eventually I felt ready to publish a few things. I had always wanted to write, but I never felt comfortable. I was never *good enough*.

As my marriage came to an end, I started volunteering and was soon consumed by that. I realize now that giving all my time away had less to do with my actual belief in those organizations and more to do with my inability to value *my-self*.

However, volunteering had benefit. I realized the world was bigger than my problems. I gained confidence in knowing I was capable and could bring about change.

With that, my passion came back. I cared less and less about how I looked and more about my commitment to the projects *I* was creating.

I stopped worrying about looking *right* when I left the house. I realized that habit robbed me of multiple hours every week, which translated into lost weeks every year.

I remember talking with a retired high school teacher when I was still spending a considerable amount of energy on how I looked. He asked me quite bluntly about how it was to be "beautiful."

He recounted that when his wife was pregnant with his daughter, he hoped that she would not be *pretty*. He had observed how hard it was for most of the beautiful girls to overcome what was expected of them and be *who they are*. He said he was relieved when his daughter was average looking.

I get that.

I still observe the same behavior in girls no matter which school we're at, or how old the girls are. And, after nearly 20 years as a feminist, I still note the same behavior occasionally in myself.

I know that my grandparents loved my sisters and me more than anything in the world. The feeling was mutual. One of my fondest memories of them was in what I considered my greatest moment of shame. At 27, I was an unwed mother. In my conservative family, this was nothing I ever imagined for myself. I remember going to their home to break the news, feeling like I had betrayed them somehow. But when I told them, they both just smiled and said, "These things happen."

There was no judgment, only love and excitement about having a great-grandchild.

Perhaps, I was the one who decided to play the princess role.

Maybe it was me who put all the pressure on all those years. Perhaps I was the one who wanted to think that staying small all those years would protect me.

Being a princess caused me to misuse nearly 30 years of my life. I now call them, "My Wasted Years as the Princess of Nothing."

"Honesty is not a social duty, not a sacrifice for the sake of others, but the most profoundly selfish virtue man can practice: his refusal to sacrifice the reality of his own existence to the deluded consciousness of others."

-Ayn Rand

I have loved Billy Joel's song, "Honesty," since I was a kid. If you browse the You Tube videos, you see Billy himself making it more and more of a *performance* through the years, and less of the heartfelt, emotional plea the song once was.

The Western world has gone down that same spiral. Everything has become one Big Show.

I listened to the song over and over again, trying to discern what is so much more dishonest since I grew up in the '70s.

> *Honesty is such a lonely word.*
> *Everyone is so untrue.*
> *Honesty is hardly ever heard.*
> *And mostly what I need from you.*

We live with dishonesty everywhere.

We have sexualized bodies up for display everywhere, but women can't pull out their natural breasts to feed their babies.

Facebook often bans breastfeeding images on their pages while allowing all sorts of other dehumanized images of women. Apparently, nothing is more offensive than a non-sexualized breast.

We Photoshop everything to the point that our kids don't even know what a real person *looks* like. Even our dolls are crazy looking. I played a game with a five-year-old girl recently where I mimicked Barbie and told her, "I'm so hungry! I'm going to eat you!" She laughed but insisted, "She's *not* hungry. Women really *do* look that way, and she's *not* too skinny."

I looked around at the other women in the room, many of whom were very fit, and saw *no one* who even remotely resembled Barbie.

However I still hear women say, "I had Barbie growing up; it didn't ruin me. What's the big deal?" The problem now is that Barbie isn't just one doll. She is *everywhere*, in massive quantities.

We contribute to this illusion by smearing make-up on our faces filled with toxins ranging from lead to arsenic, all in the name of looking "pretty." We shave our legs, our pits and our pubes as if we were still little girls instead of grown *women*. In case you haven't noticed, Barbie is completely *hairless*, in addition to being completely out of proportion. If you want to have a grown-up doll, with curves and makeup, she should be realistic. However, pubic hair would be considered *obscene* on a doll.

What is *really* obscene is that these dolls have been marketed and purchased by the *billions* since 1959. I for one have never bought a Barbie for my daughter. But I routinely throw them away in batches of five to six.

Willa Cather's phrase "an orgy of acquisition" continually comes to mind every time I attend a birthday party. Who needs five Barbie's? Who needs *one?* We talk about not having money for schools but where is the truth in *that*? The money is there, but we misspend it on crap to re-create this cycle of insanity.

We eat genetically engineered food so that we don't have to deal with our apples turning brown after we slice them.

In fact, our entire food supply is becoming so unreal that "Lunatic Farmer" Joel Salatin recently stated:

"Many think our culture is approaching the zenith of food production through genetic modification, chemical fertilization, and factory farming, when these things are actually the beginning of collapse..." (*The Sun Magazine,* October 2012)

In short, we don't honor ourselves—or even *life* itself. We worship *fantasy*.

For me, honest living means refusing to dye my hair and pretend to be younger than I *am*. It means refusing to remove hair that is there for a reason. It means not spending 15-minutes straightening my hair every day. It means not *covering* my face with makeup. It means not living in a house or driving a car I can't afford. It means leaving the unflattering pictures of myself up on Facebook anyway, because really, *who the f*ck cares*?

The Body is Not an Apology has a feature I really appreciate: "Bad" Picture Monday. Women send in pictures of themselves at their "worst." It's refreshing and surprisingly beautiful.

It's sad to think that the most political act most women now engage in is being truly *themselves*.

We have become such a self-absorbed nation that the political is now almost entirely *personal*. We forget the consequences of our apathy on the world at large.

We are too busy watching an average seven-hours-a-day of television to care that we are killing people the world over. Pakistan. Afghanistan. Iraq. Palestine. Somalia. Yemen.

Drone attacks kill *people*.

Usually brown *Muslim* people.

They often kill civilian women and children.

Acknowledging that Muslims are somehow *less-than* in our national consciousness would be a first step toward truth telling. Until we get to a point where we value *all* children equally, we will still be dropping bombs. We will still turn our backs on the millions around the world living in poverty that we helped create.

Perhaps this focus on making everyone look the *same* has caused us to devalue those who *don't*.

We don't know what is real anymore. TV and video games begin the desensitization of our children early. The military has used video games to recruit and train for years.

If there is an honest way to kill someone, it should be face-to-face, as a means of self-defense. Not at the end of a remote control button. At what point do we say, *enough?*

Honesty is not making excuses for yourself, an abusive partner, or a country that has less than a stellar history. It means speaking out. It means calling people on their bullshit.

It means not working in a job you hate to pay for things you really don't need.

It means spending time with your children instead of buying them shit. *Listening to their stories. Relating to them. Sharing your story. Answering questions honestly when they ask you.*

Honesty comes from listening to yourself and others, and saying "I don't know"—when you *don't*.

It means owning your sexuality and not faking pleasure or orgasms.

It means eating food that will support your body and not deplete the Earth in the process.

It means not taking or hoarding more than you need.

It means saying *no* when you mean no, and *yes* when you mean yes.

It means telling your partner what you *really* need instead of making them guess.

It means allowing your children to tell you what they think, no matter what their age is, or how "inappropriate" it is.

I'd rather have them get their frustrations out now than let them build up slowly until their teen years—and then snuffing them out with drugs or alcohol. I tell my kids, "You have a *right* to talk back to me. You have a *right* to tell me I am *wrong*. Perhaps, *I am*. You have a right to have your *own* opinions and feelings."

When children cannot talk to or relate to their parents, bad things happen.

It's not surprising that truth is hard to find. We socialize our kids from the get-go to be *polite*. We suppress their gut instincts about people to make ourselves more socially acceptable. No one wants to have the "disobedient" kid. Believe me, *I know*.

We must get beyond worrying about dirty looks and actually *be* parents. Parenting is not about producing a robot. Parenting is giving your children the tools they need to survive and live contentedly.

People don't like to hear the truth. They are not used to it. What we forget is that someone who tells us the truth is doing us a *favor.* How many people smile to someone's face and complain to everyone else about how moronic they are?

Honest women in particular are usually called *bitches*. We are cut off. We are ostracized. The fear of that alone keeps many of us silent.

> "We have been socialized to respect fear more than our own needs for language and definition, and while we wait in silences for that final luxury of fearlessness, the weight of that silence will choke us." -Audre Lorde

I believe when you really care about something or someone, you tell the truth.

At some point, all of this dishonesty will catch up with us and tank the Western world as we know it. Our lifestyles are not sustainable. We our building our society on the individual lies we tell ourselves day after day.

We must begin a collective change, but that can only come when we start telling the truth about our individual lives. The small white lies take time away from what matters. They add up and rob us of *actually living*.

Do I get it right all the time? No—o*f course not*. None of us do. And my version of "the truth" may be different than yours.

However, I hope to come closer to complete honesty and move away from this goofy reality show our country has become.

It is our quirky uniqueness that endears us to others. The large crooked nose, the horrendous chuckle, and the inability to put down the cookie jar.

People remember the dead for their *realness*. Attend any funeral and you will know that to be fact. No one will remember which masks we wore to be appeasing.

"Healing begins where the wound was made."
-Alice Walker

There is a wound in the world that is specific to women and girls. Many of us take a lifetime to figure out what it is.

Every person is born of a woman, but somehow the traditional creation myth was turned around on its head. Women are secondary, if not cursed, via this tradition.

The textbooks that our children read are still almost entirely male-dominated and filled with male accomplishments. Our spiritual communities are still mostly male-led and refer to God as "He." Religious thought seeps in early and is very damaging to girls. If God is a man, and "He" is everything that is good and superior, it is easy to conclude that we as women are, in fact, beneath men. Whether one practices a religion or not, this attitude has a profound effect on our collective thinking.

If you still doubt whether this is important, ask yourself why women today own only 1% of the world's wealth. That means that men, mostly white Western men, own the rest. Women, by and large, are still dependent on men for that 99%.

If God is male, men are considered superior.

And women are, therefore by default, *inferior.*

Sadly, I heard this message loud and clear, growing up in a Christian home. I vowed that my kids would be raised differently. But I've learned that "one-house-at-a-time" is not quick enough for the change we need.

I believe we often overlook children when we speak about social change. Children are the last people we should forget about because they are the future. And, when you read a child a story again and again, you transform the consciousness of both the parent and the child.

The divine female is unconventional. She does not belong to any one faith tradition. In fact, she belongs to all of them.

She does not come to us as a Savior; rather she is the force within us who empowers us to save ourselves. She loves indiscriminately; you do not have to be good to merit her attention. As Mary Oliver reminds us,

> *You do not have to be good. You do not have to walk on your knees for a hundred miles through the desert, repenting.*

So many women are still waiting for their fathers or husbands to sign their permission slips—whether it is for an abortion, birth control or schooling. This has been our indoctrination for thousands of years, so there is no blame in that. When we feel the sense of the divine within us, we learn that we do not need permission for anything. Many of the "rights" we are fighting so hard for are already things we innately possess.

When we recognize, both individually and collectively, our value as women, the world will change. The image of a masculine God is built on patriarchy, which is a vision of control through violence, whether actual or implied.

When we return to the divine female, we will stop trying to "save" women in other countries and realize that we have problems of our own to conquer. We will rediscover our rich herstory. We will realize that each of us is capable of becoming our own savior.

"Divorced men are more likely to meet their car payments than their child support obligations."

-Susan Faludi

The discussion of money is extremely important when looking at women as co-dependents. Even the word suggests something about our relationships, which I believe is based on the economic imbalances between men and women.

Until we have complete income equality, women will be dependent on men, or pay the consequences. This results in women remaining in abusive relationships.

Certainly, men can also be co-dependents. But it is a different type of co-dependency.

Our goal as "co-dependent" women must be to heal ourselves so that we can attain economic freedom from our addicted husbands and partners. Because women are often economically dependent on men—particularly when we are raising young children—it is often not possible to be completely independent, particularly in the U.S. where they don't often enforce child support or offer other benefits.

After more than a decade in the mortgage industry, working in finance became an ethical dilemma for me. I had always felt good about my work and considered myself to be an honest broker. However, I became aware that there are no "honest brokers" because the entire industry is corrupt. Even if I never directly cheated a client, the banks cheat everyone.

I earned my MBA and went into the industry because I was told my passions were not realistic or profitable. In a sense, *I sold out.*

I'm sure there were lessons learned and a reason why I spent 13 years in this industry. That said, I wish I had begun what I consider my "life work" earlier. I cared more about being successful and pleasing my family than following my own dreams.

Leaving was very empowering for me because I was finally acting on my own behalf.

Our society worships money. This means that women stay in horrible marriages because their husbands make good money. Or, women stay in jobs they hate because they want to have designer purses and nice cars.

The fulfillment aspect of life is missing; a sense of community is lacking. People are so busy trying to keep up that they aren't able to help anyone else or pursue their own dreams. Women are not likely to be handed over their half of the pie. There are two options: work harder at man's game, or abandon it altogether.

Feminism of the "Lean In" variety is about working harder and smarter, but I don't believe most women can work this to their advantage. Most women are not working in high-powered positions in corporate America.

I believe women should abandon a game that is structured in such a way that they cannot win. We should support each other's work more. We should abandon corporate products that poison the earth and other women while depleting our wallets. Women not only earn significantly less than men, they also spend significantly more on their "upkeep." This results in most (single) women dying completely broke.

There are ways for women to exist happily on their own terms but they require a bit of creativity and soul-searching.

I don't believe in accepting "life on life's terms." I have come to believe those terms are usually built on patriarchal conditions that do not benefit females. I want MY life, on *my* terms.

Yes, sometimes that's hard when your ex owes you more than $60,000 in past due child support and court-ordered attorney fees. But God damn it, I am finally living as close to *my* terms as possible.

"Only when we feel our feelings and recognize why we have them can we know what gives our lives meaning... Once we can act upon what is true for us, our choices shape our lives, and our lives are expressions of what genuinely matters to us. Only then are we free of the ring of power."

-Jean Shinoda Bolen, *The Ring of Power*

Money is usually the realm of men. Churches (also typically the realm of men) have no problem suggesting a 10% tithe, but women who put their heart and soul into feminist work are often 1) broke, and 2) afraid to ask for what they deserve.

I've also heard numerous women criticize other "successful" feminists for "making money off feminism." This has to stop. Women in *all* professions, including those who work for the liberation of women and girls, deserve to earn at least a living wage.

I spent a long time in the mortgage industry scrutinizing the finances of all sorts of people so the topic of money does not scare me. Money comes and goes. I know that all too well personally. I've been fairly well off and I've been dead broke. I've yet to get rich off feminism. I don't know anyone who has. Most of us volunteer our time (full-time, part-time, or all-the-time) to ensure the world changes for our daughters and granddaughters.

No movement can be successful without money. We live in a capitalist society. Capitalism and interest *are* evil. My years in the mortgage industry and as a single mother cemented that for me. No one in their right mind who understood an amortization schedule would ever refinance their home again—let alone even *think* of using a credit card unless their life depended on it.

That said, we still have to gain a basic understanding of how money works so that we can use it to our advantage.

We will always be considered inferior to men if we don't bind together and rediscover our power. Since we are behind in nearly every way economically, we must carefully consider the money we do have.

Marielena Zuniga wrote a brilliant paper that will stop anyone in their tracks who says feminism is not necessary. It's entitled "Women and Poverty."[7] Here are some startling statistics:

- "It is estimated that the gender wage gap costs the average full-time U.S. woman worker between $700,000 and $2 million over the course of her work life."
- "The UN estimates that globally women's unpaid care is worth up to $11 trillion dollars annually. A woman's time spent as an unpaid caregiver restricts her ability to perform paid work or to migrate to higher paying jobs. Not having a paid job also makes her economically dependent on someone else."
- "The disparity in employment between single mothers and fathers, the gender wage gap that inevitably affects employed single mothers, and the fact that many single mothers do not receive child support contribute to the high rate of poverty amongst female-headed households. In 2010, 31.6% of American households headed by single women were poor. In Canada, 51.6% of single-mother families live below the poverty line."
- "More than 70% of all elderly persons living in poverty are women. The wage discrimination and caregiving responsibilities inflicted upon women in their earlier years makes them more susceptible to poverty in their later years. This susceptibility is exaggerated in developing nations where

---

[7] Zuniga, Marielena. "Women & Poverty". Revised September 2011.
http://www.soroptimist.org/whitepapers/whitepaperdocs/wpwomenpoverty.pdf

women typically experience a lifetime of working in the informal economy or at home as an unpaid caregiver."

When I set out on my new path after my divorce, I had to cut back my expenses significantly. Everything that was not essential had to go: my car, my smart phone and my personal upkeep. The fact is, I could not afford to live my dream while primping the way I had for most of my life.

As Ruth Calder Murphy recently wrote, *I let myself go.*

> "There's a phrase—an insulting, snide, sneering sort of a phrase—that tends to be preceded by the word "She":
>
> *"She's let herself go."*
>
> "She's let herself go" usually means that, as she's aged (whoever "she" might be) or as time has gone by, or since the last time we saw her and assessed her appearance, she's somehow become less attractive, less well-kempt, less physically acceptable, somehow, and that she really ought to have done more to fight the decline."[8]

In my case, the letting go was radical. I stopped shaving anything, quit dying and straightening the hair on my head, stopped wearing makeup most of the time and quit buying new clothes altogether. All those things are expensive—and are mostly "female" expenses that we are still expected to keep up despite the still-there and substantial gender pay gap that exists across the globe.

In my case, it was *freeing*. I never realized how much time, energy and money all this upkeep took. As Germaine Greer wrote, "...if a woman never lets herself go, how will she ever know how far she

---

[8] Murphy, Ruth Calder. "Letting Myself Go". *Elephant Journal*, March 2015.

might have got? If she never takes off her high-heeled shoes, how will she ever know how far she could walk or how fast she could run?"

How true. I never would have finished *one* book. I would still be chained to my ideas of what I "needed to have" at the expense of working nonstop at a job that I hated in high-heeled shoes. I would be too drained to do anything creative or fulfilling.

As a mortgage broker I wore expensive suits to work paired with designer bags and shoes. I spent a great deal of time and money on my hair and makeup. I spent a lot of my financial gains on personal upkeep—I played the part and looked the part of a successful career woman. I made good money as a mortgage broker. But I also spent it and my divorce drained anything that was left in my 401k.

These days, I wear comfortable hand-me-down jeans and sweaters and rarely look in the mirror.

When we give up the idea that our self-worth is dependent on how we look, we stop buying into all the makeup, hair products, new clothes, etc. that cost us thousands of dollars every year. We are talking about a $7-billion-dollar-a-year industry in the United States alone that profits on women's low self-esteem.

I don't spend money on most of that any more. I spend any extra money I have on supporting women's projects, books and CD's— or reinvesting in my own projects.

It is crucial that we support each other spiritually, emotionally and economically. Just the simple task of buying a feminist book penned by a woman is an investment in yourself, your children and your grandchildren. It also supports a project that empowers other women and enables the creator to continue her work.

It also gives women more ability to break apart from the systems that support the gender pay gap. When women open their *own* businesses, they have more flexibility and opportunities for growth and income. That said, I'd also like to look at how our giving to patriarchal religions drains time, money and resources from us as well.

When I was going through my divorce, I started taking my children back to the progressive church that my grandparents attended for more than 30 years. Initially, it was because my grandmother needed a ride to church every Sunday. It was important to her and I enjoyed spending this time with her near the end of her life. We made a day out of it, going for a long lunch together after the service and then helping wherever she most needed it. I made many friends there in the process, and we kept attending even after my grandmother passed in hopes of providing a strong community for my children to grow up in.

However, I fell into a trap of giving more of myself there than I could really afford to. My energy was already at one of its lowest points as a single mom to two young children and my finances were limited at best. I felt pressure to give money I didn't have. And I felt enormous constraints on my time as I became drafted to the Christian Education Committee, and then Moderator-Elect and the "Straw Boss" of a successful Strawberry Blues Festival.

While I was happy to do this work at the time, looking back it was enormously foolish of me and I came to resent these demands of my time. My unpaid labor could have been used to get a full-time job that would better support me and my kids. I was not in the position to be a full-time volunteer. It seems to me that the role of a church should be to support single mothers, not drain them further.

Later, when the male pastor would go on to verbally abuse several female members of that church—the same man who collected a hefty salary while many of us women slaved away for free as volunteers—few people batted an eye. I lost my respect for the entire organization and some of the people inside the church as well. This soon came to include the regional and national headquarters of that same church. No one in a position of power backed the abused women; and as a woman who had given so much of myself to this church, it *stung*.

Monica Sjoo & Barbara Mor posed a searing question near the end of *The Great Cosmic Mother:*

> *"The burning question remains: Why do women continue to give our gifts—of spiritual devotion, of impassioned energy, of mental brightness, of profound social concern—to male-dominated and male-defined religious institutions which are based, structurally and ideologically, on a searing contempt and hatred for women? Why do women continue to give our physical endurance and biological endowment to patriarchal churches which exist, ontologically and practically, by attempting to dominate and control human female reproduction like a bunch of cattle breeders controlling the fertility of their cattle? What would happen, today, if all the millions of religiously active women on earth just walked out of their patriarchal churches, just left them flat?"[9]*

That's exactly what I did! I sent a resignation letter in to the entire church board and left. I began to devote my time and energy to *my* projects. I am proud of the results.

When you look at the financials of quite a few of the world's largest religions, they are in stark contrast to how most of the world lives. Almost half the world's population lives on less than

---

[9] Sjoo, Monica and Mor, Barbara. *The Great Cosmic Mother.* (Harper & Row Publishers. 1987).

$2 a day. Seventy percent of those people are women.[10] It's extraordinarily difficult to reconcile that with the stockpile of money that many patriarchal religions are sitting on.

Women as a group don't have a hefty budget to promote feminism—which *is* a doctrine that could uplift billions of people. I think that women are much better off lifting themselves and their children up than continuing to support patriarchal religions financially.

> *"In today's world, thousands of children starve to death every day; millions more suffer the kind of malnutrition that permanently damages the brain and the body. The priests of the world's major patriarchal religions—Christianity, Islam, Buddhism, Hinduism—do not consider this situation particularly "moral," but they do not consider it abnormal either. "The poor are always with us, "life is hell," etc. — the situation just seems to illustrate these priesthoods' biophobic case. In their ontological world-hatred and doctrinal nihilism, the "holy men" try to persuade us, and no doubt themselves, that suffering is the eternal and definitive human condition— and the daily starvation of children is just one more sad but inescapable example of our "mortal condition," of "fleshly sin and corruption," of samsara (the sorrow and impurity of the world), of "life on the wheel" of Buddhistic illusion. Male priesthoods of patriarchal religions—all of whom life in the maximum comfort and even luxury their cultures can afford— have been rationalizing the suffering of others for so long, throughout four thousand years of unctuous droning, no doubt they've come to believe their own words—for want of hearing anything else." –Monica Sjoo & Barbara Mor[11]*

---

[10] "Almost half the world's population, 2.1 billion people, live on less than $2 a day. Of these people, 880 million live on less than $1 a day. " - World Development Report, World Bank, 2008.

[11] Sjoo, Monica and Mor, Barbara. *The Great Cosmic Mother.* (Harper & Row Publishers. 1987), p 371.

I believe women need to radically reconsider every single dollar they spend. My hope is that feminists will begin to really think about money—as strange or foreign as it may feel to us.

If we want our message to really spread and take root, we don't have another option.

Recently it seemed likely that one of the few remaining feminist bookstores in the U.S. was going to have to close its doors. Several hours before their Kickstarter campaign was due to wrap up, I lamented about it on my Facebook wall. I was told by numerous people that I should, basically, just *wish it weren't so.*

The fact is that woman-owned businesses, writers and artists need money to survive. No amount of *wishing* is going to change our fate as women. We have to wake up and take action before our women-sacred spaces and businesses are gone. We have to reallocate the often limited funds we have as women if we truly want to see changes in women's lives globally. We have to take political action before we lose more of our Goddess-given rights. As Roseanne Barr said, "The thing women have yet to learn is nobody gives you power. You just take it."

Systematic economic oppression underlies all other oppressions. We must begin to take an honest closer look at how religion and money work *together* to oppress women. Sister Joan Chittister wrote:

> *"Women have been locked out of full humanity and full participation in religious institutions and society at large. This marginalization of women masquerades as 'protecting' them and even 'exalting' them. Instead, these attitudes serve to deny the human race the fullness of female gifts and a female perspective on life. As a result, women make up two-thirds of the hungry of this world. And women are two-thirds of the illiterate of this world. And women are two-thirds of the*

*poorest of the poor, because they lack access to the resources and recognition men take for granted. **That's not an accident. That is a policy**—one supported by religious institutions that call such discrimination 'women's place' and 'God's will.'"*[12]

Our homes mirror the patriarchal reality we learn in our churches, mosques, temples and synagogues. Therefore, it is no surprise that when women leave destructive relationships with abusive men, they are punished financially, and there are few laws to protect them. We need to find a way to ensure that ALL women and children receive the child support payments they are entitled to.

We have to find a way to make our cultures acknowledge, value and reward care-giving. Riane Eisler has spent years of her life studying just how to do this.

We must demand that there is no more wage gap. According to *A Woman's Nation Pushes Back from the Brink: Facts and Figures*, "Closing the wage gap between men and women would cut the poverty rate in half for working women and their families and would add nearly half a trillion dollars to the national economy."[13]

We must ensure that **no woman,** anywhere in the world, enters her crone years in poverty. These are the years where we should be reaping her years of knowledge and wisdom. The crone should be relaxing and reflecting on her glorious life—not slaving away at McDonalds worrying about how she is going to pay the rent!

We cannot accomplish any of these goals if we do not understand how money functions—and most importantly, if we don't work

---

[12] Chittister, Sister Joan. "Are Women Devalued in Religions?" *The Shriver Report: A Woman's Nation Pushes Back From The Brink*. January 12, 2014.

[13] "A Woman's Nation Pushes Back from the Brink: Facts and Figures" *The Shriver Report: A Woman's Nation Pushes Back From The Brink*. January 12, 2014.

together. Our individualistic lives are killing us. We need to fight back—*hard*.

We can't change everything *today*, but we can find creative solutions to make our individual and collective lives easier. We can live communally, share resources and refuse to spend one penny on anything that does not empower us as females.

Until we have economic equality, I urge you to consider how you spend your money. If you go out to eat, go to a woman-owned restaurant. If you buy a book or a CD or a piece of art, make sure it's been created by a woman. Every-single-place we spend our money has the potential to change our world.

No one sums this up better than Arundhati Roy:

> "Our strategy should be not only to confront empire, but to lay siege to it. To deprive it of oxygen. To shame it. To mock it. With our art, our music, our literature, our stubbornness, our joy, our brilliance, our sheer relentlessness—and our ability to tell our own stories. Stories that are different from the ones we're being brainwashed to believe."

We *can* refuse to participate in our own economic subordination. If we work collectively, we can also reallocate the money that runs the world in a way that works for *everyone*.

"Who taught you to hate yourself from the top of your head to the soles of your feet? Who taught you to hate your own kind?"

-Malcolm X

When I was a young girl, someone scraped most of my insides out and took them for himself. Last time I saw him, I still gave him a hug and pretended everything was *fine*.

I think I've spent most of my life looking for my insides but I never thought to ask him to give them back to me. Now I'm not sure if I want them back or not. I'm not sure if I even can ask him. I don't think I can bear the additional burden of his denial.

This scraping of my insides gave me the idea that I always had to give the very best of myself to someone else and not save anything for me. I've been eating rotting, second-hand leftovers all my life.

If my very insides were entitled to someone else—a man—how could I dare ask for anything outside of myself?

At times it seems both unbearable to continue to live this way and impossible to really change anything.

At the water park yesterday, I noticed one way we indoctrinate gender early on: bathing suits. Boys have their longish shorts. The girl option seems limited either way: a bikini that's often sexualized or a one piece that covers the entire torso. Personally, I like the sun over my entire body. If I had it my way, I'd always bathe nude. I'm long past a proper 'bikini body' but further past giving a shit. I like the feel of the sun on my breasts without the intrusion of fabric to block the sweat rolling off them.

How odd that men have the option of hiding so much more behind their shorts while women are so vulnerable in their suits with their fat and folds sticking out all over the place. My Norwegian husband is old enough to remember when boys and girls in his country just wore Speedo bottoms. I don't know what the women wore.

When I was an "acceptable woman," I still looked like a little girl and I didn't have any fat sticking out anywhere. But now I look like a "real woman," and I hate it.

I thought I loved my body until I started gaining weight. Now I realize that, much like my father's love for me, my self-love was always conditional. I glance at the extra seven pounds distributed down my back and in globs of fat on my stomach and breasts and I hate myself. I hate every spare inch of me. For someone who doesn't own a scale I still seem to always know exactly how much more space I've dared to take up.

Sometimes I want to take an old toilet brush and just scrub out all the residue deep inside of me that just won't go away.

My mom thinks feminism makes me depressed. My dad thinks feminism makes me angry. I think the way things were stacked, I'd be both anyways.

My friend Lisa says that people who can cry are brave and strong but I hold it in most days because when I do cry I feel like I have failed somehow. I feel wasted from crying. I feel so exhausted by my life that I don't dare spend extra energy on tears.

When I was a little girl, I cried a lot. My dad used to sit beside me, and rub my back for an hour without saying one word. He seemed utterly confused by me, as if I should just accept my allotted fate. I never knew why I was so angry at him, but I knew I wasn't allowed to show it. Now I know it was because he did and said nothing. He didn't try to change anything for me. He didn't stand up for me. He set me up to fail and then blamed me for feeling 'sorry for myself.'

It took me 38½ years to yell and scream at my dad. It took me 38½ years to tell him he was *wrong*.

When my son was eight years old, I sat down with him and worked out the projected comparative economics of his and my daughter's entire lives. I realized something that day: the math is our map.

We set girls up to fail economically from day one and then minimize it, like it doesn't count. When I did the math on the projected income disparity between him and his sister, they ended up more than a million dollars apart at the end of their lives. I asked my son how he would feel if he were in her shoes—and that I knew about the discrepancy, and still did *nothing* to change it.

He started to cry. He said he would feel like I didn't care about him at all.

I sat and watched him, not allowing myself to feel anything because I knew if I started crying it would go well beyond an acceptable lesson for an eight-year-old. He was crying over the million dollars—the sum at the end when it was all tidied up. Most of us can't allow ourselves to feel the little dings along the way.

The math doesn't tell you how it feels to be a single mom with less than a dollar in the bank. The math doesn't tell you how badly it stings to lose your home without the luxury of tears. The math doesn't tell you how much it sucks to have to deny your children while your ex-husband lives in a 3,800 square foot house and wears a different pair of Gucci loafers every time you see him.

Life is fucking hard for women everywhere and we're not even allowed to swear about it.

It's draining to always be polite; to navigate your words in the most-possibly-kind-way and still be called a "bitch."

It's more exhausting to *care*.

Sometimes it's all I can do to get dinner on the table and keep the house relatively clean. *Is this what happens to us? Do we just get too worn out for one-more-burden?*

Lately I feel like all the light has been drained from my eyes.

I often feel alone and angry that there aren't more people working to change things. But then I think, how can I ask anyone to join me when I feel so bad myself? *Is it easier to just give in and accept the roles assigned to us from birth?*

The way we socialize girls continues to fuck us over. *It's so insidious.*

Being raised as a girl teaches us to be raped without screaming or remembering so that it can be done day after day in every possible way without the threat of revolt. By the time we are women, most of us are either too tired or too damaged to do anything about it.

We must radically change how girls are raised from birth. It's so much easier than this never-ending un-doing most women seem to be stuck in. Just that alone is a full-time job. *Something has to change.* It shouldn't be that hard just to be. It especially shouldn't be so hard to live as a feminist, on our own terms.

But it is. It's soul-crushing work.

When my daughter turned seven, she started telling me that a Goddess lived inside her. This Goddess was so vivid to her that she decided she would write a book about Her.

I don't remember what was inside me before it was stolen. For a while, I thought it was enough that my daughter had this Goddess and I could live vicariously through her.

The thing is, I want all girls to keep their Goddess. I don't want any more boogiemen taking what is rightfully ours.

I used to feel resentful toward feminists because I felt like they weren't, as a group, doing enough to prevent this from happening to the next generation of girls. I felt like the children were forgotten; or at least a *very low* priority. I couldn't understand why we keep rehashing these same vicious cycles year after year. Now I feel, perhaps, a bit of the why. We cannot protect or nurture what we don't have ourselves.

I want my insides back.

Perhaps it took me this long to realize that I deserve them.

"May my hives bloom bravely until my flesh is aflame
and burns through the cobwebs."

-Robin Morgan, from "Monster"

These last years, I have tried to put as many women's words out into the land of social media as possible. I feel it is critically important to hear quotes by women and in particular, women's stories. *We have spent so much of our lives absorbed in the narratives of men.*

Increasingly, I am realizing that we also need to come back into our bodies and reclaim them before the words can fully sink in.

When I was trying to cope with the relapse of my ex-husband and our subsequent divorce, I began to read a lot. But in retrospect, it was Kundalini Yoga that saved my life and my sanity. No amount of knowledge could cause me to take the actions I needed to. I had to reconnect with my body and my soul.

I have recently hit another tough spot in my life. I have tried to learn more, to read more, to re-read what has worked before. But my mind does not seem capable of absorbing any of it. There is a huge disconnect.

I was fortunate to grow up with an full-figured mother who never criticized my weight. I feel a relative acceptance to this body of mine, which is one of the greatest gifts my mother gave me.

What I have realized lately is that I have become disconnected from this body of mine. It's like it doesn't really belong to me. I suppose most of us have been taught that from the get-go with unwanted or forced hugs from relatives or the incest that is prevalent in so many families or the rapes or threat of rape that June Jordan so eloquently speaks of in *A Poem About My Rights.*

In my haze of raising children, keeping up a house, working, volunteering and everything else the modern mother does—mostly alone—I have turned on auto-pilot. I shovel in food without tasting it. I never "have time" to do my beloved Kundalini Yoga. I push the classes I want to take to the back burner because my needs always come last.

Many years ago I went through Patricia Lynn Reilly's wonderful book of vow-making, *I Promise Myself*. I composed a vow of faithfulness to myself along with my dear friend Kristie. It's an excellent process that I recommend to all women. However, like any relationship, you must continue to honor your vows or it will break down.

My relationship with myself has all but stopped.

The vows that are always hardest for me to keep involve honoring my own body. This is heartbreaking to recognize because it is this body that houses my soul, and I believe the spirit of Goddess that resides in each of us.

Awhile back, I received an email from a lovely woman in the UK who is putting together a body affirming calendar for women. She wanted me to compose a quote for her to use in the calendar. Surrounded at the time by sick children, I was not inspired to write anything, so I sent her back a few quotes from other women I admire, including one from Sonya Renee's poem which inspired her movement: *The Body is not an Apology.*

> "Praise for the body, for the body is not an apology. The body is deity. The body is God, the body is God. The only righteous love that will never need repent."

I've always loved the entirety of this poem. Women have so much body hatred that it has become a multi-billion dollar industry. Dr. Gail Dines is quoted as saying, "If tomorrow, women woke up and decided they really liked their bodies, just think how many industries would go out of business."

I'm long past supporting woman-hating businesses such as hair dye and poison-riddled anti-perspirant. However, it occurred to me that while I try to support as many women I can with my purchases, I have denied both myself and businesses that are affirming of women's bodies. I have absorbed the message that I am unworthy, and on some level, *wrong*.

June Jordan comes to the close of "A Poem About My Rights" with these words:

> I am not wrong: Wrong is not my name
> My name is my own my own my own

It is the defiance in her tone of the reclaiming of what has been essentially set aside for everyone else that brings me to tears with each reading. The thing is, most of us have been told so many times that we are not entitled even to our very own bodies, that we must continually put our hands up and say, NO. Some of us may have to do this several times a day until it become natural again.

> "Daughter of Woman, your healing task is not to become a new, improved or changed person. Rather, it is to reclaim your natural and essential self in all its fullness. In the very beginning, you remembered yourself. You came into the world with feelings of omnipotence, not inferiority."
> -Patricia Lynn Reilly

We need to go back to our natural states—as children and manifestations of Goddess Herself—instead of trying to continuously improve ourselves by using outward measures.

What I believe is dangerous for women about New Age thought is that it often allows women to remain passive; which is likely why this train of thought is so popular and so profitable. While I strongly believe in the power of women casting spells—particularly on themselves—there is a difference between witchcraft, which is active, and New Age thinking, which is usually passive.

Likewise, I am not certain that we can affirm ourselves into loving our bodies, although it can help. It can be a first step. I believe we need to take action—whether it be jumping into the water naked with a bunch of other women like the calendar project—or taking a self-defense class, doing Kundalini Yoga at home or savoring a meal. We have to stop telling ourselves to love our bodies and actually live our lives in a way that *is* love. We must love and worship our bodies as if they were the Goddess Herself.

So, here is the quote I gave to the calendar maker. These two sentences encompass all my previous vows to myself. I hope it will cast a spell on women—myself included.

Your body is Goddess in one of Her most beautiful forms.
Love Her fiercely.

"There is a poem in my throat that is not yet ready to be born. But when it is, I guarantee you, it will change the world. At the very least, it will change me."

-Mark Gonzales

Long before I fell in love, I listened to India Arie sing "I am Ready for Love" more times than I can count. I became intentional about the sort of love and the sort of life I wanted to have.

List-making saved my life. I was gas-lighted so often in my second marriage I soon doubted my own reality and truth. It was only by beginning to make lists that I was able to see clearly again.

I started with a list of things my former husband had done. There was no emotion in it—just a simple list of facts that soon became over four pages. Soon he was no longer able to trick me into believing his reality. My next lists were about how to leave the relationship, how to care for my children and how to create the life that I wanted out of the shambles that were left. Eventually I composed a list of what I required in a partner—and this list birthed the most remarkable relationship of my life. It was actually the first relationship I had that contained no remnants of abuse.

Some of us are not sexually or physically abused, but quite a few of us are—far more than what the statistics tell us. Almost all women are emotionally, verbally abused or gas-lighted in some way. Many of us, I would argue, are also financially abused, but few of us realize it. I feel like a lot of Goddess circles like to keep it positive and not talk about these "downers" but I do not believe Goddess can fully emerge until we do.

Our individual and collective abuse as women keeps Her buried. Until we uncover this abuse, and bring it to light, I don't believe we will see the change we need so desperately.

My spirituality is one of action: the warrior Goddess who will fight for each of her children. She is the warrior of activism. It is this vision of Goddess who empowers each of her daughters and gives her the tools to be successful in life.

When you look at the aspirations of most patriarchal traditions, it is submissiveness (in females) that is usually valued. And submissiveness hurts us all. I remember being told specifically as a girl, that if someone tried to rape me, I should just let him because it would be easier than fighting him—and he might kill me afterwards if I tried to fight. To a somewhat lesser extent, our submissiveness training teaches us to do the same with emotional and verbal abuse. It often seems so much easier to just let it slide, or to minimize it.

Looking back, I think it was an attempted rape that I did manage to fight off that was the last straw for me in terms of leaving the Christian faith. While I was still blamed for this violence in the same ways most women are, I had an intense awakening that I had been lied to about not fighting back. Fighting back saved me from a much worse fate. Recent studies have come to a similar conclusion.[14]

It was that same year that I first learned about Goddess. I forgot about Her for some time, in my yearning to get ahead after college. But when my daughter was born I realized if I didn't return to Her, I would fail my child in the same ways I had been failed.

The easiest way to squash the Divine within each woman is to abuse her, whether that is physically, sexually, emotionally, financially or otherwise. As women are rising to their Goddess-potential now, we have a responsibility to our younger daughters to both nurture and protect them. Traditional patriarchal laws do not protect women and children.

---

[14] Straus, Tamara. "Teaching women to fight today could stop rapes tomorrow." *Quartz* (June 11, 2015).

I have been pleased lately to see the non-traditional ways women are taking care of their own, whether it be Gulabi Gangs, Warrior Sisters or the mother who recently went viral on You Tube—with more than 60 million views as I write this—after her ex-husband was only sentenced to 90 days of jail for sexually abusing her daughter. She successfully named and shamed this perpetrator in a way that he will never escape from. I believe we must fiercely protect our daughters—biological or not—from predators. The time of abusing women and children—and getting away with it—is over.

"We do not grow absolutely, chronologically. We grow sometimes in one dimension, and not in another; unevenly. We grow partially. We are relative. We are mature in one realm, childish in another. The past, present, and future mingle and pull us backward, forward, or fix us in the present. We are made up of layers, cells, constellations."

-Anaïs Nin

I have a hard time with speaking. The mandates of quietness and submissiveness that I grew up with in the church still plague me as a 40-year-old woman. While I *can* speak when pushed, it is still something I find extraordinarily difficult. I could actually go days without saying one word to anyone. Having youngish children doesn't make that an option for me; nor does the fact that I am *desperate* to end the patriarchy that has strangled me since birth.

I want a very different life for my daughter.

I still feel a cringe factor when it comes to Christianity, my faith of origin. Admittedly, there is still a gaping wound there; my (Christian) father and I have not spoken for more than a year. Our differences in opinion regarding faith and feminism play a big part in that.

In addition, I have been in the midst of a traumatic family court situation that seems like it will never end.

My sisters—of all faiths—sustain me. Muslims, Jews, Goddessians, Atheists, and Christians. Throughout the last six months, I've had conservative Christians and Muslims praying for me and witches casting spells and lighting candles. I've cried my heart out to women of all faith persuasions and have been supported in different ways by each of them.

When I went through my second divorce seven years ago, I was at my lowest point ever. I had shrunk to a nearly invisible size and was barely functioning. I had no legal representation and no money. I did the best I could with two young kids and very little help. My children helped me to realize that I needed to become my strongest self again.

Feminism gave me the vision that I deserved better; my faith gave me the strength to persevere until better came.

Today, I sit in the courtroom with the attorney who has been representing me for the last six months. We have spoken before about his son, who I know he adores, but I have not fully comprehended WHY he agreed to take on my case, now totaling tens of thousands of dollars with my measly $200-a-month payment. He gives me the why in code that I decipher in my head. He mentions singing in a choir, which ultimately leads me to ask him more. I like this style of his; he doesn't beat me over the head with the fact that he's a Lutheran. And so my questions begin.

I'm quite sure he doesn't identify as feminist—but his act of charity to me as someone whose reality is mostly that of a single mother—certainly is. *It is an act that no one else over the last eight years has been willing to do, male or female, feminist or not.*

I sit nervously in my chair, fingering the tiny gold charm inscribed with *Al-Fatiha*, silently reciting the verse in my head as I nervously make it through the court proceedings. While I rarely do the things that most people associate with Islam anymore, it is these moments in my life when I rely on my faith to sustain me.

During these last trying months, I often questioned the potency of my feminist work under the rock I felt stuck under. I worried that I was not able to adequately protect my own children—or even myself for that matter—under our patriarchal system. I'd ask myself, *who am I to speak of these things when I can barely hold my own head above water?*

The truth is that I could not have won my case—or my life back—without the help of this Christian attorney. The truth is that it's unlikely I would have stayed sane these last years without the support of my secular humanist husband. The truth is that I would be utterly lost without the support of my sisters around the world of *all* faith persuasions. Had I locked my heels and refused to be open to the possibilities of who *could* help me, I would likely still be trapped in the same miserable spot.

In those moments in the courtroom I began to question my resentment of Christianity and reconsider what it means to actually be a Christian—or a person of any faith.

I grew up with a pamphlet that listed the supposed beliefs of nine other major religions (summarized in a brief paragraph), followed by detailed explanations about why each belief was *wrong*. My religion was fundamentalist Christianity and I followed it to a T. Looking back, I am embarrassed to say that while I knew people from a variety of cultures and religions, the only reason I ever spoke to them was to convert them.

As a teenager, I read *The Book of Mormon* and started going to Seminary, again with the intention of saving *those poor Mormon kids*. The missionaries came to my home in droves, two-by-two in their white dress shirts and ties, where I often confounded them. No one could answer my never-ending questions.

I suppose the Muslims were the most concerning to me then, although I didn't read the Qur'an until college, after marrying a Muslim. At that point, I *had* to read it, because everyone was *certain* that my *savage* Arab husband would soon start beating me.

A few years earlier, I had left home to attend a Southern Baptist college with the intention of becoming a minister. It soon dawned on me that the *real* purpose for girls in that school was to find a husband.

Once I began to study the historical, linguistic, and cultural roots of the Bible in-depth, I felt as though I had been lied to my entire life. I left Florida nine months later an atheist, certain I could never believe in anything again.

Back home, I found feminism and a cute Lebanese guy. Both would change the course of my life forever.

I never had any intention of converting to Islam. My new husband encouraged me to think on my own terms and believe in myself – which was something completely new to me after growing up as a submissive church girl. It was that freedom and the kindness of my new family that prompted me to study Islam. It wasn't so much the Qur'an itself I was in love with; I still find it a boring and tedious read. What drew me to Islam was Ramadan—and the dream of full equality between all people.

One thing that has always stuck with me since my conversion is that the way people viewed me completely changed. I am still the same person I always was, but suddenly I started hearing that I "deserved to die" and was a "sand nigger." After 9/11, I was also told that all Muslims "should be put into internment camps."

Every single week, I hear racist, shitty comments about Muslims —often from other feminists.

Many people forget that racism and sexism are brothers.

Approximately one quarter of the world's population is Muslim— and few, if any, people ever leave their faith of origin. Islamophobia only guarantees that the majority of Muslim women will be isolated, resentful, and suspicious of the Western world.

There is a general feeling in many Western feminist circles that women of faith cannot be feminists. This is particularly true of Muslim Feminists, but I've certainly seen it with other groups as well. For example, when Kate Kelly was excommunicated from the

Mormon Church for speaking out on her views about the treatment of women in that church, I often posted to my Girl God Facebook page about her situation in solidarity. Time and time again, I heard a similar response: "She should just leave that church."

I do not share that view. The "should" is deeply concerning to me. Certainly there is value in challenging the patriarchal structures from within, too. I would argue that we have no hope of saving the world via feminism if we ignore the belief structures that saturate the planet.

Faith is often cultural. It involves entire families and communities; hence faith is deeply personal. While I don't regularly practice Islam anymore, it is hurtful when I hear other feminists make comments about Muslims. My first marriage didn't work out, but it had nothing to do with religion and everything to do with getting married too young. My Lebanese in-laws are still family and my first husband remains a dear friend. Over the last 20 years, I have maintained friendships with Muslims in my local community, and increasingly, all over the world thanks to social media. I *love* my extended Ummah.

While there are certainly things that I would challenge about the Muslim faith, it is not helpful to receive such criticisms from those who know little about Islam. I liken this to the dynamic in many families that it is OK to critique your own family members, but when someone outside the family starts shredding the character of a mother or sister, all hell breaks loose.

Religion tends to be divisive and women (especially feminists), cannot afford to be divided anymore. Life is so much harder than the Disney movies many of us grew up watching. It is deeply unfair to women, and particularly unjust to women of color. Nothing prepares most of us for the reality of our daily lives. We need each other now more than ever.

Gerda Lerner wrote that "Men develop ideas and systems of explanation by absorbing past knowledge and critiquing and superseding it. Women, ignorant of their own history do not know what women before them had thought and taught. So generation after generation, they struggle for insights others had already had before them, resulting in the constant inventing of the wheel."

I believe a big part of that problem is that women within feminism are fragmented and don't take the time to listen to each other often enough. There is so much that we can learn from each other to avoid reinventing the wheel every generation. If you tear a blanket up into bits, it no longer functions as a blanket. But if you sew those same pieces back together, you can still keep someone warm.

There are obvious remnants of misogyny in all the world's religions. Women, still, for the most part are not equal participants in the leadership of most faiths. The expected submission and subordination of women and girls continues to be the norm worldwide.

When I read Patricia Lynn Reilly's *A God Who Looks Like Me,* I wished that there was a similar book for Muslim women, but I didn't know of any. When I wrote *The Girl God*, I wasn't sure I'd find the divine female within Islam at all. I was pleasantly surprised to find Her everywhere.

My spirituality has changed drastically *many* times over the years as my life has coursed through three husbands, two birthed children, and many other radical changes. I have moved far away from a male God and shifted toward Goddess Spirituality.

Feminism is also a faith—a faith that someday, somehow, things will improve for at least our daughters and granddaughters. My dream is that life will change for the better for us, too.

Many of us are still learning to speak in our own words. We must be patient with ourselves and with each other as those words come out.

"When we own our stories,
we get to write a brave new ending."
-Brené Brown

Family court zapped me. I mean, it really took a good ten years off my life. The six months in court and the several months before court (anticipating what would happen) aged me enormously.

Sadly, to this day, my ex-husband has never even begun to complete any of the court-ordered mandates that would allow him to spend time with his children. They have not seen their father for well over a year now. This is both enormously sad and simultaneously more peaceful. There is very little drama in our lives now.

After court, I remained somewhat stunned for at least a month. Looking back I can see that I was just getting by. I put out an anthology—but that period is mostly a blur for me. There is nothing quite so traumatic as the fear of losing your children.

I received notice from my landlord that he wanted to sell the bungalow we were living in about two weeks after court ended. It was pretty much a shithole of a place but he had been somewhat flexible and we lived in a neighborhood that we adored. It had been a good home for us for more than two years.

I *really* did not want to move again. My credit was still tanked from my divorce—and it was difficult to find a landlord who would take me in between that and my inconsistent writing income and spotty child support payments. Somehow it had not hit me yet that I could take my children and move to Norway—as my dream had been for over four years. One day while I was sitting around trying to figure out what to do, I realized that *perhaps* that was an option. I pulled out the 40-page judgement and went through it line by line.

> Mother is awarded sole legal and physical custody of the children, subject to Father's reasonable parenting time as set forth in Exhibit 1 attached hereto. Mother's residence shall be the children's usual place of residence.

> Mother is awarded sole custody and will make all major decisions regarding children. Mother is encouraged to consult with Father regarding major decisions; however, Mother shall have full decision-making authority.

The last 25 pages were devoted to the conditions by which my ex could have access to his children. In the previous six months, he had completed none of these requirements and did not show up for the last hearing at all. It seemed likely that these conditions would never be met.

My hands were shaking as I went out to my mom's trailer and told her. *I couldn't believe it.* I had to have her call the attorney to confirm it.

Once that was sorted out, I decided we would move to Norway right away. I did not know then *for sure* that my ex would never follow through on the court-orders, but I had a good inkling. I decided we would move and worry about it later *if* he got sober. *We had been waiting on him long enough.*

I started making lists of everything in our house we needed to sell or give away. I began selling the things we could do without first. We held onto our dinning room table and my mattress the longest. I spent hours taking apart my son's double bunk bed the week before we left. I planned to have a two-day yard sale but it ended up being 3-4 days in the very hot Portland sun. I was completely exhausted and sunburnt. I would send my son out for food. My daughter remembers eating ice cream one morning for breakfast but I have no memory of that.

My mom found a place to live nearby and moved there. We paired everything we owned down to four suitcases and our carry-ons. My daughter had the hardest time with it. My son and I were less attached to things so we gave her more room in our suitcases.

I finally rented a Zipcar and took the four large suitcases over to my first husband's house. I had called and asked him if we could stay with him until we left. At that point we didn't even have airline tickets and I didn't know when I would have the money for them. He said we could stay as long as we needed to.

When I arrived there I must have looked like a mess. His friend didn't recognize me at first. After we left, Hussein later told me he said, "Man, *what happened*? I feel sorry for her. She used to be so beautiful."

We spent a last night in our house which was terrible. Some people who had said they were picking up large items didn't. We literally lived in the hood, and our last nights reflected that more than any of the previous years. We had a crazy man try to beat down the front door and a visit from the police.

The next day we spent with my next door neighbor and her family. All the neighbors came to say goodbye and wish us well. The next morning she drove us into downtown Portland with all our carry-ons. We walked through the city with all of them, waiting for a friend to get off work. We found a fantastic street musician by a water park and I listened to him for hours while the kids played.

Finally we boarded a MAX train to an old friend's house, rented a Zipcar the rest of the way there and stayed with her for four days. She took us to the beach one day, but mostly we relaxed at her house. We managed to get a final dentist visit in so my son could have all his teeth fixed before we left. She dropped us off at Hussein's and we spent the rest of the week with him.

Hussein's three children are like cousins to my children. He lives on about two acres so it was the perfect setup. The kids were occupied and happy. I cooked—and he barbequed—and we all ate well. Hussein would usher me over for coffee breaks every so often. We had some very good talks.

Anders called mid-week after finding three tickets for us that were not horribly priced. It was a 27-hour trip—but we finally had a way there. He sold a velomobile that helped with the cost.

It was hard to say goodbye to Hussein. He is the closest thing I have to a brother and I knew it would be some time before we met again.

My children's paternal grandpa had offered to drive us earlier so I decided to ask him if he was still up for that. The ride there was pleasant enough and he even gave me a hug when they dropped us off.

My mom met us at the airport. We had a fun time with her before we had to go through security. We flew to Philladelphia overnight. We stayed there about four hours and then flew to London. We arrived in the middle of the night and nothing was open.

By the time we went through customs, my daughter was literally dragging her nine-year-old body all over the filthy floor. I could not get her to stop despite everyone glaring at us. I was now carrying most of the carry-ons and was too tired to care.

We finally made it through the line after about an hour. We hoped to find food but could not find any. My ex mother-in-law had packed us very generous food packages but by then the cheese and sausages were no good and had to be thrown away. I was about to just forget about it when my son spotted a M&S store in the distance. It was a beautiful store filled with lovely food that we normally would not splurge on. We pigged out and watched cartoons all night. I thought we would sleep on the flight to Bergen but none of us did.

When we arrived, my husband was there with my oldest stepson. They took all the luggage and we took a van cab home. My husband ordered pizza and my other stepson joined us for an early dinner. By 4 PM we all crashed until the next morning.

When we woke up it was *freedom*. My husband must have been at work; I can't remember now. I took the kids down to the center of our little suburb to walk around. I don't remember much about those first weeks other than how *good* it felt to finally be in Norway.

We now live a life without constant conflict and stress. My husband is a true partner. When we left our first parent-teacher conference meeting, I started crying as we walked out. I never had this level of support from my children's father.

We spend our days together in a modest home filled with musical instruments. It was a bit crowded when we got here, but we have de-cluttered and made adjustments so that everyone has their own space. Money is tight—but we eat, sleep, and love well in the Bergen rain.

I haven't been called a nasty name in a *very* long time.

It took me a while to get used to that.

Epilogue

"The past must be examined closely, I believe,
before we can leave it there."

-Alice Walker

One might wonder why I chose to publish this book—particularly after reaching a good spot in my life.

I had planned to wait until my children were grown and try to put all of this behind me in the interim. However, even after nine months of bliss in Norway, I still was not feeling *well*.

I kept reverting to old patterns, long after I knew *intellectually* how to live better. The past, it seemed, wouldn't die without me taking a good long look at it.

Upon reflection, I realized that I had often chosen (on some subconscious level) to be around dysfunctional people who created constant drama. It was my way of avoiding the trauma in my childhood—and dealing with it.

When I came to Norway, there was no more drama. Anders is practically a saint, having never said one unkind word to my children or me over the last five years. Even when I tried to start an argument with him, he would respond with love.

I no longer had any distractions; so I plunged myself into my work. I self-published four books and a calendar within my first year here.

While working on *New Love*, I had some painful realizations and unblocked some of my repressed memories of childhood abuse. I burst into hysteric sobs several times on Anders' shoulders. I began doing some critical reading of my own—some of the same books I was recommending to others via my work. *The Courage to Heal*, *The Body Keeps Score* and *Trauma and Recovery* were a big help to me.

If I were to write out a narrative from my twenties, it would be quite lively and long, but none of it would have any particular meaning or make much logical sense. I had a lot of *fun*, if you can call it that. I lived out of a premise that I was "liberated" from my fundamentalist Christian background—by *what* I don't know—I suppose you could call it "liberal feminism." I theorized that I was taking back my body from those who had tried to steal it from me in my earlier years. Giving it away to everyone else certainly wasn't reclaiming it for *me* though. I had to find ways to repossess myself in ways that truly were liberating and healthy. That has taken me a *very* long time.

My great grandmother used to tell me, "If you don't have any regrets, you haven't lived!"

I have plenty of regrets, and I've certainly lived an interesting life thus far. (Sometimes a bit *too* interesting.) But I have learned, and grown, and died and bloomed again.

I regret deeply how I treated my first husband at the end of our marriage. Although he forgave me long ago and encouraged me to forgive myself—I often wonder now how much I was punishing myself all those years in the karmic belief that I somehow deserved to *pay*.

There is no logical reason why I should have ended up with my second husband. *We never fit.* Even if I was terribly misinformed about addiction and naive about drugs, people were always puzzled about how we ended up together. Some have theorized it was about the money. *I don't think so.* When he was at his best, he treated me like a princess. And there was something completely irresistible about that.

However, being a princess is a trap. It is only by discovering the Goddess within us that we can heal and thrive.

Raising my daughter caused me to re-think everything about my life and how I had been raised. Five years ago, sick with "princess culture," I angrily wrote on my Facebook wall:

> Do you want your daughter to be a Princess or a Goddess? Princesses usually have no mother, are forever submitting to their father and spend all their time looking good for and finding "Prince Charming." Goddesses are powerful in their own right and can do whatever the f**k they want! #ChangeHowYouSpeakToYourDaughter

It took me a few years to transfer that to myself—and realize how deeply ingrained princess culture was for me growing up in the seventies and eighties.

Despite decades of feminism, every sort of self-help book, an MBA, and a strong career, I remained trapped in a view of myself as helpless. *I was still waiting for my Prince to come save me.*

That belief only buried me deeper into sinking sand.

Becoming the Goddess of my own life was about stripping everything away and starting from scratch. I left my money, my credit, my "good looks," my career, my house, my car, my cell phone, my pride, my core beliefs, and every toxic relationship behind.

In short, I was in hell for more than a decade.

I spent a lot of nights crying myself to sleep and divorcing myself from people, places and things that no longer served me. What emerged was my Goddess-essence. I can't say that life is always easy or perfect, but I am finally in a healthy and loving relationship—and my children finally have an opportunity to heal and thrive.

After spending the better part of 15 years working toward "recovery," I have to wonder why the onus is on *women* to recover instead of on *men* to stop abusing us in ways that necessitate our recovery.

Self-help is obviously an industry—one that is primarily targeted at women. *And what do we need the help for?* There is nothing intrinsically wrong with being female—although we are certainly made to feel that way from birth.

In my case, I was seeking self-help to recover from male violence.

We know statistically, if we look, who is committing violence on this planet—and it is primarily males. Why don't men stop verbally, physically, sexually and financially abusing females?

Men not only get away with this on a *massive* scale—while often still being lauded as "good men"—but females are then left with the mess of trying to recover from their abuse.

In retrospect, I would advise my younger self to be much more selective about what sort of people I gave any of my time or energy to. And there would be fewer males in that mix.

While we cannot completely protect ourselves from rape and murder, we do know now from looking at patterns that most abuse happens at the hands of men who know us—perhaps who even claim to *love* us. I think we should—both individually and as a community—cut these men off completely.

I used to think that all male-female relationships had some element of abuse in them. I had built up defense mechanisms since childhood to protect myself from that. I now know after being in a relationship now without abuse that it is *not* actually a component of *all* relationships. I have had to replace my unhealthy behaviors with new ones—which is not always an easy or automatic task. Embracing Goddess has helped me through that.

Goddess has been a guilty pleasure of mine for the last 20 years, although it wasn't until my mid-thirties that I was able to fully embrace Her. She had been hidden and demonized throughout my childhood in a way that took me a long time to get over.

Once she was fully unveiled, there as no turning back on the rage that I felt and the power that slowly returned to me. This awakening cost me several of my primary relationships. Despite the loss that I felt, I could not revert to the person I once was. I had to live in the power that I intrinsically *knew* instead of pretending to still be weak.

Goddess does that. Once your eyes have been opened to what has been suppressed, you cannot close them again. Hence, *most men are scared to death of Her*. Having a safe place or a sanctuary is critically important for those of us who are awakening to Her reality.

For many people, Goddess is still a New Age fantasy. It is easy to dismiss Her for this reason alone. Goddess scholarship is therefore *critically* important. Women and girls need to understand Goddess as a historical reality. There is a reason so many go to such lengths to suppress Her. It has taken me a lot of digging to find Her.

When Adrianne Rich wrote, "You must read and write as if your life depended on it," she was certainly speaking to me. There was a least a year that I did little more than the basics of caring for my children. The rest of the time, I spent reading everything I could— and then cried my eyes out writing out my pain and loss.

Working with Arna on *New Love* was a healing journey for me as well. I come from more of a radical feminist perspective while she gets me to embrace some of the neuroscience that helps with my own healing. While we were finishing that book, I realized I needed to go back to my past and un-bury some of the trauma I had stored in my body.

I went back to an anonymous blog I had kept as a means to leave my second marriage. I was shocked at how much I had shut out from my memory.

I thought I had written perhaps about 150 pages altogether on my blog. Going through it and taking out the highlights, I ended up with more than 800 pages. My mind was blown away at all the things I had blocked out.

When I began this book, my back literally felt as if it were breaking every day.

What I realized in committing all of this to a book is that my deepest shame was that I had been unable to protect my children from their father for so long. I saw the way they continued to struggle and suffer and I blamed myself, mostly.

As I was going through my divorce, I was unaware of the structural misogyny that keeps so many women in the same damned spot I was for so long. I have since come to realize how fortunate I was that my ex's addiction problems were so severe that the judge ruled in my favor. I have since met dozens of women who have lost their children to abusive men in the "family court" system. We need to change that system, swiftly and radically.

I wrongly assumed that writing this book would be a simple, cut and dry process. It was the hardest of all my books for me to complete. I cried *a lot*. I lost my shit several times. I realized that I truly *am* a warrior Goddess.

I attempted to keep the blog text as close to the original as possible, although at times it is choppy and hurts my ego as a "writer" and "evolved person." When all is said and done, I feel that's a more honest portrayal of my journey. I hope your ride was a bit less bumpy than mine was.

Mona Eltahawy said that, "The most subversive thing a woman can do is talk about her life as if it really matters." Claiming this is harder than one would think. My life *does* matter—and so does yours.

Thank you to all of you who have stood by me in big and small ways all these many years. I love you.

Early versions of some of these chapters appeared in *Return to Mago, Love, Inshallah, Over the Moon* and *Elephant Journal*. I thank the editors for their generous support.

Enormous thanks to my mother, Pat Daly, for editing this book. I know that there were parts that could not have been easy for her to read through, and I struggled with whether I should even ask her to complete this difficult task. In the end, I knew this book could not exist without her enormous skill-set. And so, I honor her as both my amazing mother and as my writing partner.

A big thank you to Tamara Albanna, Nicola O'Hanlon, Susan Morgaine Stanley, Rhonda Case and Karen Brzezinska for taking early looks at the drafts, which were often rough and patchy.

Many thanks to Arna Baartz for allowing me to use her gorgeous art on the book cover—and for being a wonderful partner on so many projects.

Tremendous love and gratitude to my husband, Anders, for holding me as I wrote the tough parts and putting up with my mood swings as I dealt with the aftermath.

This book is dedicated to anyone who has been affected by alcoholism, addiction or abuse. It is my attempt to break the destructive cycle that has plagued me for most of my life.

Shortly after this book was released, my ex lost his long battle with addiction. Quietly sobbing alone the dark morning after, he came to me, wrapped his arms around me—and told me he was sorry.

I believe him this time. This world was a very hard place for him, too. I hope he finds the peace in the afterlife that alluded him in this one.

I release this book, not with malice, but with the hope that it will help other women get out of hell sooner than I did. Abusive relationships cause immense suffering to the body, mind and psyche long after they are over. And we do not help our children by passively remaining in them.

May we all heal, grow and prosper. And may our children find better ways to celebrate "this thing called Life."

Suggested Reading

A Deeper Wisdom: The 12 Steps from a Woman's Perspective – Patricia Lynn Reilly

A God Who Looks Like Me – Patricia Lynn Reilly

All About Love: New Visions – bell hooks

Beautiful Boy: A Father's Journey Through His Son's Addiction – David Sheff

Be Full of Yourself: The Journey from Self-Criticism to Self-Celebration – Patricia Lynn Reilly

Beyond God the Father: Toward a Philosophy of Women's Liberation – Mary Daly

Breaking Down the Wall of Silence: The Liberating Experience of Facing Painful Truth – Alice Miller

Chakra Balancing – Anodea Judith

Clean: Overcoming Addiction and Ending America's Greatest Tragedy – David Sheff

Communion: The Female Search for Love – bell hooks

Cunt: a declaration of independence – Inga Muscio

Emerging from Broken; the Beginning of Hope for Emotional Healing – Darlene Ouimet

Going Out of Our Minds: The Metaphysics of Liberation – Sonia Johnson

Gyn/Ecology: The Metaethics of Radical Feminism – Mary Daly

Her Best-Kept Secret: Why Women Drink-And How They Can Regain Control – Gabrielle Glaser

I Promise Myself: Making a Commitment to Yourself and Your Dreams – Patricia Lynn Reilly

Imagine a Woman in Love With Herself: Embracing Your Wisdom and Wholeness – Patricia Lynn Reilly

In the Realm of Hungry Ghosts: Close Encounters with Addiction – Gabor Maté

Liberating Motherhood: Birthing the Purplestockings Movement – Vanessa Olorenshaw

Loving to Survive: Sexual Terror, Men's Violence & Women's Lives – Dee R. Graham

Make Your Creative Dreams Real: A Plan for Procrastinators, Perfectionists, Busy People, and People Who Would Really Rather Sleep – Sark

Many Roads One Journey: Moving Beyond the 12 Steps – Charlotte Davis Kasl

Matri: Letters from the Mother – Zoe Ann Nicholson

New Love: a reprogramming toolbox for undoing the knots – Trista Hendren & Arna Baartz

Of Woman Born: Motherhood as Experience and Institution – Adrienne Rich

PaGaian Cosmology: Re-inventing Earth-based Goddess Religion – Glenys Livingstone

QUINTESSENCE: Realizing the Archaic Future A Radical Elemental Feminist Manifesto – Mary Daly

Sister Outsider – Audre Lorde

Sula – Toni Morrison

The Body Keeps the Score: Brain, Mind, and Body in the Healing of Trauma – Bessel van der Kolk MD

The Courage to Heal: A Guide for Women Survivors of Child Sexual Abuse – Ellen Bass and Laura Davis

The Dance of the Dissident Daughter – Sue Monk Kidd

The Great Cosmic Mother – Monica Sjoo & Barbara Mor

The Holy Book of Women's Mysteries – Zsuzsanna Budapest

The Obsidian Mirror – Louise M. Wisechild

The Real Wealth of Nations – Riane Eisler

The Verbally Abusive Relationship: How to recognize it and how to respond – Patricia Evans

Trauma and Recovery: The Aftermath of Violence–From Domestic Abuse to Political Terror – Judith Herman

Victory Over Verbal Abuse: A Healing Guide to Renewing Your Spirit and Reclaiming Your Life – Patricia Evans

When God Was a Woman – Merlin Stone

Why Does He Do That? Inside the Minds of Angry and Controlling Men – Lundy Bancroft

Women, Sex, and Addiction: A Search for Love and Power – Charlotte Davis Kasl

You Can Heal Your Life – Louise Hay

Additional Resources

AVA Project runs courses and training for organizations and individuals supporting families through Domestic Violence, and they have a number of online courses and tool kits that could benefit women experiencing DV themselves. There are also links there to other major UK charities and organizations that offer advice and practical support.
http://avaproject.org.uk/our-resources.aspx

Resources for **Divorcing a Narcissist** (One Mom's Battle):
http://onemomsbattle.com

Domestic Violence Solutions: http://dvsolutions.org

Emerging from Broken: http://emergingfrombroken.com

Emotional Freedom Technique: http://eftuniverse.com

Free Radical Feminist Book Downloads: (Andrea Dworkin, Mary Daly, Audre Lorde and many more!)
http://radfem.org/category/various-authors

I Love Recovery: http://iloverecovery.com/

Imagine a Woman International: http://imagineawoman.com

Men Ending Verbal Abuse and Control (MEVAC) has a very thorough, free program for rehabilitation of male abusers. (This is also very private with provisional levels of membership, phone verification, and required reading and writing to be done by the man in order to get access to full support). http://mevac.proboards.com

Online Support Groups and Resources for **Suicidal Thoughts:**
http://theicarusproject.net/node/25274

The Icarus Project: a support network and media project by and for people who experience the world in ways that are often diagnosed as **mental illness**. "We advance social justice by fostering mutual aid practices that reconnect healing and collective liberation. We transform ourselves through transforming the world around us. "
http://theicarusproject.net

Verbal Abuse Site by Patricia Evans: There are some good resources, including a very private online support group (you have to call to get added). http://verbalabuse.com

Women for Sobriety: http://womenforsobriety.org

If you enjoyed this book, please consider writing a brief review on Amazon and Goodreads.

www.thegirlgod.com

61901206R00155

Made in the USA
Columbia, SC
27 June 2019